Serious Fun

The Power of Improvisation for Learning and Life

Ruth H. Yamamoto

Hamilton Books

An Imprint of
Rowman & Littlefield
Lanham • Boulder • New York • Toronto • Plymouth, UK

Copyright © 2017 by Hamilton Books
4501 Forbes Boulevard, Suite 200, Lanham, Maryland 20706
Hamilton Books Acquisitions Department (301) 459-3366

Unit A, Whitacre Mews, 26-34 Stannary Street,
London SE11 4AB, United Kingdom

All rights reserved
Printed in the United States of America
British Library Cataloguing in Publication Information Available

Library of Congress Control Number: 2016952943
ISBN: 978-0-7618-6853-8 (pbk : alk. paper)—ISBN: 978-0-7618-6854-5 (electronic)

♾™ The paper used in this publication meets the minimum requirements of American
National Standard for Information Sciences Permanence of Paper for Printed Library
Materials, ANSI/NISO Z39.48-1992.

This book is dedicated to:
John, Duncan, and Walker, who support me,
albeit with good natured ribbing.
And the improvisers of the world, who support each other.

Contents

Contents

Preface

I credit my junior high school drama teacher, Judy, with beginning my journey into the wonderful world of improv and for helping me to become the person I am today. I was in junior high when improv was incubating. Judy not only had the foresight, but also, the courage to include improvisation in her curriculum, which some theatre arts teachers today do not do. Additionally, Judy partnered with a local professional theatre that had an outreach improv group called *Living Stage*. My classmates and I lived for the days that *Living Stage* came to work with us. In between, we played and had our own improv troupe (overalls, rainbow shirts, or rainbow suspenders, and all). Some of us would get together and perform on the Mall in Washington, DC with a jar in front of us. It was the era of *Monty Python* and *Saturday Night Live*, and this drama teacher had given us a toolbox with which we young people could emulate these funny people. I did not realize, at the time, the value I would place on the skills I had learned. We just thought we were having fun.

When I reached high school, I was unpleasantly surprised that my high school drama teacher did not include improv into her curriculum. My junior high fed two high schools and divided our improv team. We tried to keep in touch and keep performing, but high school priorities and life took over. Interestingly enough, my high school generated at least four big name stars. One of which was a contemporary of mine who went on to be a star in spite of our high school drama teacher. While I did not go on to stardom, I do not feel a failure. I attribute that to improv. I feel I always have my toolbox with me.

Fast forward many years, after trying my hand in professional theatre, I decided to go back to where it was fun. I decided to teach theatre. The adage "those who can't do, teach" is rubbish. I became a teaching artist and believe my students benefit from my experiences and passion for my art. I am still surprised that so few theatre arts educators include improv in their curriculum. Furthermore, I do not understand why improv is not included across the curriculum when researchers have added credible evidence of the benefits. With this book and the study, it describes, I hope to add to the pool of credible evidence through scholarly research of the serious benefits that lie within the fun of improv.

Acknowledgments

My acknowledgements begin with the sources of the ideas, which made up the framework for the study in this book:

The improvisational giants on whose shoulders all of us who love improvisation stand: Viola Spolin, Keith Johnstone, Augusto Boal, Jonathan Fox, and Del Close.

The theorist and brilliant psychologist, who developed the concept of flow: Mihalyi Csikszentmihalyi.

The play scholars, who believed in the value of play for life: Stuart Brown, Brian Sutton-Smith, and Peter Gray.

Thanks to my family and friends, who have supported me financially, emotionally, and physically. These people I consider as my *backline*, always there to make me look better and help me when my scene might be failing.

Thanks to the participants of the study, who graciously shared their time, spirit of fun, and love of their craft of improv. I hope this study lends credibility to the practice of their art.

Thanks to John Flohr and Cheryl Keen, who were my chair and methodology faculty at Walden University. Their guidance, patience, and kindness got me through my doctoral journey.

Thanks to Judy Thibault-Klevins and Dan McSweeney, who shared their passion of their craft and inspired me to teach.

Thanks to the applied improvisation professionals, who volunteered to be interviewed for this book: John Windmueller, Lisa Safran, Rebecca Stockely, Chris Sams, Michelle James, and Sue Walden.

Thanks to those who contributed to my GoFundMe campaign to get this book to print.

I

The Origins

Chapter One

Introduction

Why Have Fun?

"Having fun is fun. . . having fun is. . . It really makes me feel great. It makes me feel better about myself. It makes me feel."
—Flynn (pseudonym, study participant)

Recently, I heard the current surgeon general of the United States say that he believed a key factor to good health was being happy. This idea contradicts or rather reverses what I, as a middle-aged adult had been taught growing up—that being healthy leads to happiness. At a time when it feels like the pressures of life outweigh the pleasures, it would seem that people have fewer and fewer opportunities to have fun. Furthermore, most learning institutions do not make it a priority to spend instructional time to teach young people how they can have fun or find fun in any aspect of their lives. Perhaps, as Americans, we have our forefathers to blame for this; the Puritan work ethic gave little room for the concept of fun as being important. Across the country, the assumption that work (be it adult or child) should be taken seriously and that anything resembling play or fun should not be. This assumption leads me to believe that those who subscribe to this idea can never be happy and, therefore, never be healthy.

To my knowledge, this is the first book to study the influences theatrical improvisation or improv had on the ongoing development of college students. The serious fun described through the study and this book is improv. It is an art form that is often overlooked, ignored, or laughed off as unimportant.

There is no question in my mind of the importance of improv. As a theatre arts educator for the past 20 plus years, I have included improv in my teachings. Mostly I did so because I knew not only how to improvise, but also, how to teach it. Unfortunately, few teachers, let alone theatre arts teachers, know how to teach it or recognize the potential for learning improvisation holds. I had one art educator colleague express an actual fear of teaching improv. This trepidation is because improv has been and still is treated as the bastard child of theatre and is often not included in theatre arts curricula. It is often viewed as frivolous and silly, which then infers that those who do improv are also frivolous and silly. What a blow to one's confidence; who doesn't want to be taken seriously?

Still, improv is becoming more and more mainstream. The television show, *Whose Line Is It Anyway?*, and sketch comedy shows such as *Saturday Night Live* and *Key and Peele* brought improv out of the comedy clubs and into peoples' living rooms. While this represents movement, it does little to legitimize the art form. I await the day for a major award to be given to a comedic or improvisational actor.

Beyond legitimizing the art form, with this study and this book I argue we, as humans, need to start infusing our education with more than science, technology, engineering, and math. The arts are simply too important to cut. They teach us to be human. They teach us how to collaborate, to dream, to enjoy life, and to have fun. Not everyone who studies art becomes an artist, but so too, not everyone who studies science becomes a doctor. The arts add to the whole person. The cost to include improvisation is minimal; it requires a room and people willing to have fun and share themselves. The cost to society for not teaching some form of improv (be it dance, music, or conversation) could be a cultural disaster.

In this book, I share the findings of my doctoral dissertation and make those findings accessible to more than just the academic world. I add my opinions and experiences as further evidence of the importance of not only improv to a well-rounded education but as a means of thinking of one's life. I studied the perceptions of college students who trained, practiced, and performed theatrical improvisation or improv at a mid-Atlantic community college. I underpinned this study with the concepts of flow (Csikszentmihalyi, 1991), man the player (Huizinga, 1950), the balance of the elements of play (Caillois, 1958), and prior writings and research of theatrical improvisation. Part One of this book sets the stage and provides background for the study. In Part Two, I present the study. And in Part Three, I discuss the implications and potential for change as indicated by the study and through interviews with applied improvisation professionals.

As a word of caution, those readers looking for quantitative, measurable data in this study will be disappointed. That does not mean that, like the topic of the study, the research itself should be taken less seriously. I argue that the data provided by the participants in this study come from reflection and introspection. The quotes from the study participants included in this book were not forced from them but rather shared with a sincere desire from the participants to share their craft and their feelings of it. With this book, I hope to add to their desire to validate the craft and lend credence to their pursuit of fun.

It is a sad state of affairs when people do not know how to have fun. Today's youth are bombarded with technology that "help" them perform any task from buying a pizza to finding a date. Make-believe games stop after kindergarten. Furthermore, in schools, educational policies dictate what students will study and how they will be tested on that material. The fun in life that many of us experienced as kids where you can find enjoyment in simple things has been quashed. The opportunities for young people to find and experience fun and to develop a system of intrinsic rewards for the rest of their lives are dwindling. And so, in 2016, we are on a threshold. Do we as educational stakeholders need to continue to drill and fill and continue to cut the arts, or do we invest in our culture and teach people how to have a little fun? Referring to the comment from the surgeon general, how can we possibly be a successful, happy, and healthy group of people if we don't?

Chapter Two

What Is Improv?

"I think in general improv troupes should be more respectful of themselves. I think that they should take it seriously and to view it as the art, as the beautiful, wonderful, scary, dirty, gross, awesome art that it is."
—Donnie (pseudonym, study participant)

DEFINITION

Many definitions exist for improvisation. In a case study presented for the purposes of understanding the cognitive process of improvisation, Magerko, Manzoul, Riedl, Baumer, Fuller, Luther, and Pearce (2009) defined improvisation as "the creation of an artifact and/or performance with aesthetic goals in real-time that is not completely prescribed in terms of functional and/or content constraints" (p. 117). Although this description serves as a good scientific definition, it does little to describe the aesthetic quality of which the researchers spoke. The why and how of theatrical improvisation is the subject of this book; I merely offer this definition as a starting point. Humans improvise without thinking about it, when they converse, when they play, when they are faced with decisions, whenever they need to generate a re-sponse or a reaction. Improvisation is the creation of new material by an individual or group immediately or without prior planning (Goldstein & Winner, 2012; Joos, 2012; Magerko et al., 2009; Sawyer & DeZutter, 2009). Alternatively, composition involves the creation of a new artifact or idea but also includes iterations and occurs over a period of time (Joos, 2012). Both terms describe modes of creativity and act as endpoints on a continuum. Many forms of improvisation exist (i.e., musical improvisation, product in-novation in businesses, and theatrical improvisation), and all forms adhere to the basic definition of improvisation (Goldstein & Winner, 2012; Joos, 2012;

Magerko et al., 2009; Sawyer & DeZutter, 2009). This definition and the idea of a creativity continuum aid the understanding of theatrical improv and guide the focus of investigations for future research. Within theatrical improv, also, exist different styles, which I will discuss next. For this book, I use the term improv to describe unscripted acting (again a very broad definition).

BRIEF HISTORICAL BACKGROUND

Prior research provides extensive samples of and background on improv history going back as far as 500 years (Joos, 2012; Meyer, 2006; Sawyer, 2003; Zaunbrecher, 2011). Rather than rehashing historical research, I will skip ahead to more recent "ancient" history, to the 1960s and 1970s. The form of improvisation that I discuss is similar to the work done by actors at Second City Theatre in Chicago, Lone Moose Theatre in Canada, Upright Citizens' Brigade in New York, and other companies around the world. In particular, Second City and Lone Moose pioneered the game-like version that can be seen today on the show *Whose Line Is It Anyway?* Second City's form evolved from Spolin's seminal work on improvisation for the actor (Joos, 2012; Sawyer, 2003). Lone Moose's Theatresports format evolved from Johnstone, as improvisation as noncompetitive games, and Boal as theatrical games for nonactors (Johnstone, 1983; Joos, 2102). Concurrently, Fox (1994) was developing Playback Theatre based on the sociodramatic work of Moreno. Although improv has been practiced and performed since the 1970s, this game-like form of improv became accessible to the general public through the British radio production in the 1980s and television broadcasting of *Whose Line Is It Anyway?* in both Britain and the Unites States in the 1990s (Berk & Trieber, 2009).

FORMS OF IMPROV

Theatre games should in no way be thought of as the only form of improv. Furthermore, not all improvisational troupes seek to be comedic. Improvisational troupes that follow the social theatre vein developed by Boal, Freire, and Moreno tend more towards sociodrama. Playback Theatre, created by Jonathan Fox, uses unscripted theatre to build community. Playback Theatre applies this type of theatre by retelling stories and connecting the audience and players through shared experiences (Fox, 1994). Through the retelling of stories and the process of improvisational theatre, people make connections and share experiences.

Making connections and sharing experiences are not limited to sociodrama or the more serious forms of improv. Perhaps this is the heart of my argument: not everything that is funny lacks value. In fact, I am arguing for just the opposite that having fun in the context of improv acts as the intrinsic reward that motivates people to participate and to continue to participate in improv—fun adds value. At the research site in this study, the participants practiced and performed primarily short form improv and theatre games that the participants described as fun. In the chapter on themes, I term this theme of attraction to the craft The Hook. The fun and the play-like quality of improv draws people in and opens them up to the potential benefits of improv.

FORM STRUCTURE OF IMPROVISATION

While improvisational actors appear to be freely creating instant scenes, a framework of rules provides the structure that allows improvisers to work (Joos, 2012; Magerko et al., 2009; Sawyer & DeZutter, 2009). Spolin (1987) presented the basic rules in her seminal work, *Improvisation for the Theater*; researchers continue to see these rules appearing in the data analyses (Joos, 2012; Magerko et al., 2009; Sawyer & DeZutter, 2009). These basic rules include trust, presence, and acceptance (Gesell, 2005; Spolin, 1987). Furthermore, the rules provide an overarching framework from which the actors work (Joos, 2012; Magerko et al., 2009; Sawyer & DeZutter, 2009). Also, each game has a set of rules, and within each group, the performers have rules for the group (Magerko et al., 2009; Sawyer & DeZutter, 2009). Joos (2012) placed improvisation, as an action, on one end of a creative continuum and composition on the other end. Theatrical improvisation has rules and a framework, much like play (Berk & Trieber, 2009). All of this structure limits the freedom of the actors but also fosters the creative environment of improv, thus putting it further away from the improvisational end of the continuum but still not on the compositional end (Joos, 2012).

IMPROV AS A NONCOMPETITIVE SPORT

With his seminal work, Johnstone (1987) stressed the competitive nature of improv only as a means to get improvisers together to collaborate and play together. In the opening to *Whose Line Is It Anyway?* the host always makes a point to note, "The points don't matter" (Hat Trick Productions & Warner Bros. Television, 1998). Boal (2002) stressed the benefits of these theatrical games to the social collective as a means of a nonthreatening way to work out problems. Boal's work tended more toward sociodrama, as did Moreno's and Fox's work. In this study, while social competencies and semitherapeutic elements emerged from the data, I focused on the game-like quality and playful nature of improv in the study. Furthermore, because improvisation is both process and product, I investigated both sides of the arguments on process versus product creativity training.

PRIOR RESEARCH

Earlier I stated that improv lacks significant scholarly investigation. This statement is partially true in that the much of the research happened over 5 years ago, the research of improv is spread over many fields or disciplines, and that few researchers approached their studies from the actors' perspectives. This section reviews the scholarly work that served as a foundation for the study in this book.

Of the theory and research on improvisation, authors of the literature indicated connections of creativity, empathy, and social competency to improvisation (De Backer et al., 2012; Gesell, 2005; Koutsoupidou & Hargreaves, 2009; Miner, Bassoff, & Moorman, 2001) and theatrical improvisation in particular (Lobman, 2003, 2005; Maples, 2007; Sawyer, 2006; Zaunbrecher, 2012). In the past, researchers studied improvisation as a method or strategy for teaching creativity and building collaborative learning environments, but only in a general sense. In looking for a deeper meaning to understand why young adults pursue and practice theatrical improvisation outside of a standard college curriculum, I reviewed literature from different fields using different approaches. The findings from the study confirmed some other findings from this vein of research. However, as previously mentioned, much of the literature predated my study by over 5 years. These theoretical articles and studies are included as they serve to underpin and describe the concepts of this study and identify areas where research happened and current research is needed.

RULES AND STRUCTURE OF IMPROVISATION

As with play, all forms of improv lie on the free play versus structured play continuum. Many people believe improv to have no structure—that it exists in chaos. That improv has no structure is untrue; the beauty of improv is that it just appears that way. Improvisation intended for performance (theatre, music, and dance) has rules and structure, which place the art form away from free play end and more towards the structured end of the play continuum. Gesell (2005) argued that theatrical improvisation must adhere to the rules of acceptance, trust, and presence. Actors and practitioners of improv have extrapolated these rules from the works of Spolin and Johnstone (Aho, 2006; Gesell, 2005; Joos, 2012; Sawyer, 2004a, 2004b; Zaunbrecher, 2011). The rules and structure inform the actors or players and provide a greater opportunity for creative thought (Gesell, 2005). Furthermore, Gesell argued the rules should be thought of as irreducible in the context of improv. All three rules are important to the art form; the art fails to happen without all three. In several of the studies I have included here, researchers noted and discussed the necessity and role of the rules of improv.

Acceptance and the" Yes, and..." Rule

In improv, actors speak in terms of making an offer; this can be verbal or nonverbal (Spolin, 1987). The responsibility of any other actor on stage is not only to agree (say *yes*) but also to extend that offer by adding *and*. Adding just *yes* does not perpetuate the scene; adding *but* is really not accepting and poses a contradiction to the offer (Zaunbrecher, 2012). The rule of *yes, and...* serves two purposes: promoting ongoing scene and play framework through which cognition happens (Wiener, 1999; Zaunbrecher, 2012). Because rules and standard structure exist in theatrical improv, the actors begin to create meaning without confusion or disagreement.

Imagine a pick-up game of tag. Most people who wish to play the game come to it with a general framework. When someone violates one of the agreed upon conventions, play stops. An example would be if tagged, the *tagee* refuses to become *it*, a violation to a basic rule of the game. No game of tag exists without an *it*. Acceptance means adhering to the framework or platform (Gesell, 2005; Sawyer, 2004a, 2004b; Zaunbrecher, 2012). The rules of the real world only exist in a theatrical improvisation if an actor presents them as such. If an actor says, "The sky is green," any other actor on stage must accept that statement and move that scene forward. If the second actor fails to do so, the audience may laugh, but the scene has nowhere to go (Sawyer, 2004a, 2004b; Zaunbrecher, 2011, 2012). Gesell (2005) noted that agreement alone is not sufficient. The key and importance of acceptance (the *and* part) allow cocreation of an environment where opposing opinions can exist. Many nontheatrical organizations, such as corporations, use this catch phrase for the reasons noted by Gesell, making it a useful life skill (O'Neill, Piplica, Fuller, & Magerko, 2011).

Miner et al. (2001) studied organizational improvisation and noted that conflict sometimes occurred between team members when improvising. In their study, the researchers investigated improvisation where the *yes, and* rule did not exist and reported an increase in conflict within the groups studied. In the field of education, Berk and Trieber (2009) argued for the inclusion of theatrical improvisation to learner-centered teaching. In a collaborative classroom, teachers who negate what students offer to the learning process stop the process and, often, disengage the students (Berk & Trieber, 2009). In a case study of preschool teachers ($N = 4$) who used the *yes, and* rule as part of their play-based classroom, Lobman (2005) noted the teachers reported development of leadership skills for and engagement of the students as evolving from this rule of their classroom play. Sawyer (2004a, 2004b) argued for the necessity of acceptance in classroom discussion as a way for the group to learn as a collective. Although many consider acceptance as the golden rule of improv, Spolin (1987) described point of concentration as another valuable rule.

Point of Concentration and Presence

Within a scene, a goal or a problem always exists; the job of the improviser is to focus on that problem (Spolin, 1987). The point of concentration provides a framework in the chaos so that spontaneous creation can occur. Zaunbrecher (2011) noted that focus could also mean the rules of the particular game. Gesell (2005) chose to argue more for the power of presence for helping to focus out extraneous factors and being in the moment. In their report of improv games used in a college mental health class, Berk and Trieber (2009) argued for the use of improv games with students of the Net Generation because of the students' characteristic tendency of overly multitasking. Berk and Trieber interpreted the rule of presence or point of concentration as being in the moment. Unfortunately, the authors did not perform a formal study, so while the findings were interesting, the validity is unreliable. However, the idea of being in the moment has real-life implications for not only students but also anyone who needs to work as a collective.

For Crooks (2007), presence and being in the moment are essential for team cohesion in the workplace. Crooks presented games of presence in sample workshop outline and stressed the importance of focusing on the rules of the games so that creativity could happen. In this way, Crooks and Zaunbrecher agreed. Nigh's arguments followed Gesell's interpretation of presence. Nigh's (2013) phenomenological study examined the influences that dramatic centering exercises, similar to some improv warm-ups, had on student development and indicated an increased capacity for collective awareness. Although the exercises Nigh investigated were passive, the concept of presence appeared a valuable aspect of the process. The students in Nigh's study reported a sense of trust between the other members that provided them with a sense of creative freedom. Interestingly enough, both sides of the debate on the role of presence spoke from the educational and workplace perspectives. However, beyond Nigh's study, these arguments were theoretical and lacked scientific investigation.

Trust

In a reflective article, Maples (2007) described incorporating improv strategies to her middle school English class in hopes of cultivating students' different intelligences and engaging them in the subject matter. Although not an empirical study, Maples' (2007) study included reflection on the outcomes she observed: most notably, increased confidence and community by the students. Gesell (2005) attributed outcomes such as those Maples observed to the rule of trust. The trust rule has two prongs. The first involves trusting the process; the second involves trusting the others in the scene or group. Having shared rules increases the ability to communicate, integrate, and engage (Crooks, 2007).

Trusting the process involves a level of confidence within the activity. Wiener (1999) argued for the use of improv in developing interpersonal skills. Although Wiener spoke from a psychological standpoint, other researchers and scholars have echoed the idea. For the rule of trust, the literature I reviewed bordered more on the psychological domain and the subjects of psycho and social drama. Trust plays a large role in therapeutic settings (Moreno, 2008). Humans generally feel more capable of spontaneity when they feel a sense of trust in the process or the others with whom they interact (Gesell, 2005). Because improvisers need to have the freedom for the spontaneity that the art form requires of them, additional research is needed to find out how actors perceive the influences of trust in their art work.

Trusting the other members of the scene depends on the reliability of fellow players (Berk & Trieber, 2009; Crooks, 2007; Gesell, 2005). A tangential rule of trust is to make the other actors look good (Zaunbrecher, 2011). Fear of failure often acts as a block; however, knowing that another person always has your back can be incredibly empowering. Beyond trusting the team, trust includes the audience. Boal's (2002) work was in social theatre where communities included the audience to help work through community problems (Moreno, 2008). Wiener (1999) argued that people without the qualities described by these rules (unaware and unaccepting) often display the opposite qualities of being shallow and self-serving. Furthermore, people who do not trust and accept often fail to fulfill ethical social obligations that promote community (Wiener, 1999). The rules of theatrical improvisational and their applications in nontheatrical situations need further investigation from the perspective of the actors for increased awareness and insight.

CREATIVITY AND IMPROVISATION

Although all art forms have been found to enhance learning, foster creativity, and promote social skills (Milgram, 2003; Reilly, 2009; Ribeiro & Fonseca, 201; Sanguinetti, Waterhouse, & Maunders, 2005; Stevenson et al., n.d.), other researchers have argued that improvisational acting produces significant gains in these areas (Goldstein & Winner, 2012; Lobman, 2005; Sawyer; 2004; Vera & Crossan, 2005). In Belgium, De Backer et al. (2012) studied the potential long-term benefits of arts education to primary education curricula. Of the three forms of arts education studied, De Backer et al. reported improvisational acting to have the highest factor loading for creativity stimulation as measured by artists within that artistic medium. With these findings, the researchers added positive input to the discussion of arts education early in a child's development and for the sustainability of such a program throughout a child's education. Unfortunately, the De Backer et al. study investigated a program inconsistent with most of the educational opportunities offered in the United States.

Sawyer (1999) described collaborative emergence as creativity that arises from a group activity. Novel ideas happen during improvisation; however, the group filters these ideas according to the appropriateness of the situation or scene, doing so together and almost instantly (Sawyer, 1999). Improvised scenes cannot be reduced or attributed to an individual performer; thus, these scenes need to be examined holistically (Berk & Trieber, 2009; Joos, 2012; Sawyer & DeZutter, 2008). With the framework of the rules, theatrical improvisers not only share mental models but also create knowledge together (Sawyer, 1999; Sawyer & DeZutter, 2008). Conversely, Zaunbrecher noted educational philosophers and scholars have examined the strategy of collaborative learning as it occurs in improvisational groups and determined this to influence the social competency and intrapersonal skills of the group members (Berk & Trieber, 2009; Goldstein & Winner, 2012; Sawyer & DeZutter, 2008). In addition to collaborative learning and development, Goldstein and Winner (2012) reported significant gains to theory of the mind (TOM) and empathy for students that studied improvisational acting over other forms of art education.

SOCIAL SKILLS

In this section, I describe specific skills as noted by authors of the literature. The researchers and authors noted in this section took different methodological approaches but arrived at similar findings. Some researchers have studied the connections between improvisation and social skills development (empathy and adaptability) when improvisational acting is used as a learning strategy and organizational tool, but not resulting from the praxis of improvisation as art work.

Empathy and Theory of the Mind

Thinking of empathy development as seen as an emergent from the process of improvisation, Ribeiro and Fonseca (2011) described the shared experiences of improvising dance as leading to the development of kinesthetic empathy. Ribeiro and Fonseca (2011) attributed this empathy to the existence of mirror neurons in the brain. Conversely, Ribeiro and Fonseca (2011) presented counterarguments that addressed the theory of mirror neurons exist in humans; these arguments hinged on a lack of observational research from the field of neural sciences. Goldstein and Winner (2012) performed two concurrent quantitative studies with elementary ($n = 75$) and high school students ($n = 28$) to determine if a positive correlation existed between acting training (improvisation) and the students' development of empathy and TOM. As control groups, Goldstein and Winner (2012) sampled music classes. Although noting limitations, which included preexistent classes and teacher reporting, the researchers determined an increase in both TOM and empathy for the high school students. Goldstein and Winner (2012) noted that the older students scored higher than did the younger ones. The researchers discussed the possibility that the older students had a greater capacity for empathy development. In rationalizing the sample for this study, I was interested to see if this could also be true of young adults at the collegiate level. Furthermore, I added to the discussion of empathy development as seen through the research and scholarly articles on role-playing.

Adaptability and Problem Solving

On an immediate level, improvisational actors have to adhere to the point of concentration rule; in doing so, actors must adapt and problem solve within the scene or games. Sawyer (2004a, 2004b) argued that improvisation strategies used within the classroom help students develop skills they need in the real world. While controversial and still not validated, Ribeiro and Fonseca (2011) used the concept of mirror neurons to describe the action of collective decision-making. Ribeiro and Fonseca noted that improvisational dancers adhered to a structure of rules within a dance and collectively problem solve throughout the improvisation. Sawyer and DeZutter (2008) noted a need for a platform or structure from which the students in their study adapted the performance material for each performance. As I investigated the meaning participants held for theatrical improvisation, similar themes of development emerged from the participants' descriptions.

Underpinning their study on prior research that connected musical improvisation and creativity in children, Koutsoupidou and Hargreaves (2009) performed a mixed method study. Koutsoupidou and Hargreaves addressed the problem of creativity training in primary school music instruction as required in the National Curriculum of England. These researchers performed a quasi-experimental intervention in which the variable was the inclusion of improvisational music instruction to the students' music curricula. All the subjects in the experimental group ($n = 12$) scored higher on the posttest on the Webster's Measure of Creative Thinking in Music II (MCTM-II) than the control group ($n = 13$). As a call for future research, Koutsoupidou and Hargreaves (2009) discussed the need to study whether musical improvisation training can affect creativity gains in other domains. In looking for other research, I could find no similar studies from the medium of theatrical improvisation. This lack of literature indicated a gap between the domains of research and provided an avenue for future research.

Social Tolerance

In addressing tolerance and theatre, the works of Boal (2002), Freire (2001), and Fox (1994) come into play. These founding artists set out to bring people together in a nonviolent manner to address social issues. Of this genre of theatrical improvisation, a different branch of research emerged. I reviewed a few studies that represented a crossover between the fields of sociology, psychology, and education. In education, this genre is called Theatre in Education (TiE). Koukounaras-Liagis (2011) researched the question of whether a TiE program in two Greek schools could positively influence students' perceptions and attitudes towards religious and cultural diversity. While the researchers determined that the TiE program provided a framework that opened the dialogue for tolerance, they were unable to determine long-term effects of the program. Within the field of psychology, researchers reported sociotheatre and psychodrama in the form of theatrical improvisation and roleplaying aided in social skills training (Wiener, 1999). Another term that gained use is *applied theatre* (Taylor, 2002). Similar to TiE, applied theatre happens in nontheatrical settings; the performers and audience share the goal of nonviolent solutions to social issues for community building (Taylor, 2002). With researchers and authors arguing for the potential gains to social skills development, a gap appeared in the form of substantive research in this area.

IMPROVISATION FOR EDUCATION

Prior researchers investigated and described how improvisation has been and could be incorporated in education both in and out of the classroom for students of all ages. Much of this literature predates this study by over 5 years. The next section reviews the literature specific to the practice of improvisation in education.

Within the Classroom

The majority of studies in which researchers investigate the phenomenon of improvisation refer to musical improvisation. Koutsoupidou (2005) concluded through statistical analysis that older teachers used musical improvisation in their classes more than younger ones who had less experience. Across the curriculum in nonarts classes, educators have used theatrical improvisation as learning and teaching strategies rather than as an art form unto itself (i.e., Maples, 2007). Furthermore, most of the literature from this perspective represents reflection or theoretical points of view. Two researchers, Nigh (2013) and Meyer (2006), performed their dissertation work on drama exercises and theatrical improvisation (respectively) within theatre arts classes. I discuss the Meyer (2006) study toward the conclusion of the literature review in Chapter 6, as Meyer's work closely resembled my study.

Outside the Classroom

One possible reason researchers have conducted so few studies on theatrical improvisation inside the classroom could be the decline of theatre arts education at the different levels of education. Policies such as No Child Left Behind (NCLB), Race to the Top, and Common Core have affected public school education to focus on core subjects such as math, science, and technology (Amrein-Beardsley, 2009; A. Johnson, 2004; J. Johnson, 2010; Kataoka & Vandell, 2013). However, arts instruction still occurs outside the classroom in the form of extracurricular activities, after school programs, and clubs. The eight articles I reviewed included a meta-analysis of after school arts programs (Stevenson, Limon, & Reclosada, n.d.), a dissertation on after school dramatic program for high school students (Stevenson, 2011), two quantitative studies with after school arts programs (Kataoka & Vandell, 2013; Milgram, 2003), and three studies at the collegiate level (Foubert & Urbanski, 2006; Graham & Donaldson, 1999; Stevenson & Clegg, 2011).

Although the study was over 10 years old at the time of data collection for this study, Milgram (2003) statistically determined a correlation between participation in non-academic after school activities (dance, drama, art, and social leadership) in high school and personal satisfaction in adult life. At the time of the study, Milgram noted limitations to the study, beyond students self-reporting, as having been strictly a quantitative study with a need for qualitative research to understand the relationship between creativity and future lives. Stevenson et al. (n.d.) also noted a lack of qualitative research in this area while stressing the potential benefits arts education programs present to the challenges young adults will face in the 21st century.

Professional Development

Maples (2007) and Lobman (2005) described benefits to educators of incorporating theatrical improvisation into the classroom; however, that involves professional development. Many educators lack the confidence to improvise within their classrooms (Jacobs, 2011; Sawyer, 2004a). Jacobs argued that all educators act and improvise when they teach. Sawyer argued against transmission teaching and for collaborative teaching as seen in theatrical improvisation groups. These observations present an area for future research: theatrical improvisation and professional educator training. Further research in theatrical improvisation would broaden the knowledge base of teachers at any level of education (K–12 or higher education).

ORGANIZATIONAL IMPROVISATION

In searching for literature on improvisation and learning, I found articles beginning in the late 1990s, which focused on improvisation, both theatrical and non-theatrical, in organizations. Scholarly works with a nontheatrical basis from the 2000s begin with discussions of ideas such as product development (Miner et al., 2001) and move toward understanding the phenomenon for artificial intelligence (AI) studies (Magerko et al., 2009). Other scholars (Gesell, 2005; Pruetipibultham & Mclean, 2010; Sawyer, 2000) investigated theatrical improvisation and theatre training methodology. Both lines of investigation noted more positive influences to performance and community building than negative ones.

Theatre arts training might offer the greatest potential as a strategy for organizational well-being (Senge, Cambron-McCabe, Lucas, Smith, & Dutton, 2012). Through theatre arts training, people internalize systemic operations that might result in behavioral changes that increase the overall functioning of an organization (Pruetipibultham & Mclean, 2010). This concept of operation adheres to Moreno's (2008) idea of a social atom reacting in unison. Miner et al. (2001) reported on the learning outcomes of improvisation; Adler (2006) noted that many business schools began including arts-based courses into the business curriculum in the early 2000s.

Nontheatrical Improvisation and Organizations

Miner et al. (2001) performed a field study to investigate if and how people in organizations learn through improvisation. While the improvisation observed in the Miner et al. (2001) study was not theatrical, the basic tenets of nontheatrical improvisation remain the same. However, research on organizational improvisation follows a framework that resembles one of musical jazz rather than one of theatrical acting, thus representing a gap in the literature with regard to theatrical improvisation (Vendelø, 2009). Although separated by eight years, Vendelø noted the same benefits to organizations as did Miner et al. (2001) regarding innovation and problem solving. Negative aspects of incorporating improvisation with organizations could include a propensity to assume that solutions devised through improvisation will work in any situation (Vendelø, 2009). Vendelø described the difficulties in studying organizational improvisation as needing to be able to quantify the phenomenon, "bring stopwatches and copies of the written score of standard of activity being performed" (p. 453). Thus, many recent researchers used a quantitative approach to study organizational improvisation that left a lack of qualitative research in the field. Miner et al. noted that future research should also include other forms of improvisation to expand the effects on things such as social competency and leadership development.

Theatrical Improvisation in Organizational Development

In addition to studies of organizational improvisation, studies have been performed (Vera & Crossan, 2005) and theoretical articles written of theatrical improvisation with organizations (Crooks, 2007; Sawyer, 2000). Crossan investigated improvisation for organizations in the late 1990s; however, in those studies, Crossan focused on the collaborative aspect of improvisation as seen in theatrical improvisation (Vera & Crossan, 2005). Sawyer (2000) added to the knowledge base connecting the fields of organizational learning and theatrical improvisation. From studies such as those performed by Crossan and Sawyer, improvisational training for businesses has developed in hopes of improving corporate team performance (Gesell, 2005). While studies from the late 1990s to mid-2000s have shifted a focus toward changes in the business world, none of the reviewed researchers indicated the transferability of their findings to education. The findings and theoretical arguments presented here of theatrical improvisation, as a strategy for education and workplace training, present compelling arguments for further investigation in different populations. In a similar vein, researchers examined the influences of play on education. Scholars and research experienced similar hurtles as theatrical improvisation scholars.

In this chapter, I reviewed scholarly work that I deemed relevant to my investigation and presented it in the hopes of enlightening others on the basic tenants of improv as identified by other scholars. The next chapter, I do the same thing for the concepts of play that I felt were part of the warp and weave of the conceptual fabric, which I put together.

Chapter Three

Play and Why It Matters

"In our play we reveal what kind of people we are."
—Ovid

The second strand of the conceptual framework for the study is play. Within the study of play, many researchers and scholars have argued that play benefits learning in areas of not only content but social competence and personal skills (Bergen & Fromberg, 2009; Dewey, 1910; Nichols & Stich, 2000; Piaget, 1962; Rasmussen & Gürgens, 2006). A lack of current research creates a gap in the knowledge of the connection between play and learning. Furthermore, despite the focus in prior research of the benefits of play to young children in education, play holds relevance for young adults in higher education as well.

THEATRE GAMES AND MAN THE PLAYER

Just that title seems to decrease improv's importance, to trivialize it. But really, what would we humans do without the capacity to improvise? We would have never gotten out of the caves and escaped the hungry dinosaurs. I am not saying that theatre games are the Darwinian solution to man's survival, but I ask you to think about it. Humans are not performing comedic sketches every moment of the day; however, the capacity and knowledge of improvisation do pervade into the small and big moments of our lives. When I began my scholarly investigation on play, I started with Huizinga (1950). Huizinga argued that *homo sapiens* was a misnomer for our species. Yes, we are wise and we reason (those sound so much more legit too). Huizinga said we should be called *homo ludens* or man the player. It takes the ability to reason in order to play. Sure there are arguments out there that animals play, and that we are not the same species, but I agree play is inextricably inter-twined in our culture. Huizinga further argued that play did not come from culture—it was culture.

BALANCE OF PLAY ELEMENTS

All activities have a spirit of play (Caillois, 1958). Caillois described the elements of play against a continuum with free play on one end and struc-tured play on the other. In *agôn*, or competition, players test themselves against others or themselves (Caillois, 1958). In mimicry, players pretend play (Caillois, 1958). Acting exemplifies mimicry in a higher education cul-ture. Games of chance exemplify *alea* (Caillois, 1958). Dizzying or exhilar-ating activities, such as roller coaster rides or skiing, exemplify *vertigo* (Cail-lois, 1958). When one element dominates or is underrepresented in a culture, humans seek to balance the elements (Caillois, 1958). Furthermore, Caillois noted that sometimes the imbalance has negative effects. In current educa-tional settings, the elements of play appear to be heavily competitive, and students have very little opportunity for role playing (mimicry). We humans have a need for play and not just as children. Through play we learn to collaborate, communicate, create, and think critically (while having fun). Big questions: Why are we not instructing more people to play in school, and when we do why is it heavily competitive?

PLAY AND EDUCATION

As a student of Huizinga, Caillois advanced Huizinga's work on play. Previ-ously, Huizinga argued that all human endeavors could be categorized into three elements of play: competitive, dizzying, and mimicry. Callous added chance to the play elements. According to Huizinga and Caillois, play also exists on a continuum with free play (*paidia*) on one end and structured play (*ludus*) on the other. Both theorists argued that all aspects of life should embody some form of play or have the spirit of play and exist somewhere on the continuum. With this logic, education and school be no exception and exhibit a spirit of play.

Role of Play

In ancient times, since they had no need for a job, only free men had the opportunity to pursue leisure activities (Huizinga, 1950). The Greek word for leisure is *skhole* or *schole*, from which the modern day word for school derives (Harper, 2001). Aristotle argued for the pursuit of leisure and happi-ness as a goal for education (Csikszentmihalyi, 1991). Plato (1994, 2009) argued for education to include the study and playing of music as equally important to the study of mathematics, dialects, and philosophy. Ancient students pursued these subjects in the hopes of attaining higher enlightenment; any other studies Plato considered only worthy of the mundane and lower class citizens (Huizinga, 1950). When Plato philosophized, he often did so playfully (Ardley, 1967). Take Plato's Laws. Plato (1994, 2009) wrote them as a dialogue between fictitious characters. The spirit of play is very evident in Plato's writings. For the ancients, the spirit and nature of education focused on play and leisure activities. At some point in history, this philosophy of education flipped. Subjects such as reading and writing took places of prominence, whereas play and playful pursuits lessened in importance in an education. In 2015, while I could identify elements of play in education, I found it difficult to describe much of contemporary education for children or adults as play. In fact, many consider school as children' work.

Process Learning

One of the major changes in U.S. education occurred during the Industrial Revolution (Senge, 2012). People began to view education more as a product than as a process. Dewey (1910, 1916) argued against such learning and for learning through doing. Similarly, Dewey (2005) extended this theory to art and differentiated between a work of art (the product) and art work (the process). Both ideas seem to involve a level of engagement and action with these activities that go beyond what has become standard in education today with transmission or lecture style teaching strategies (DeZutter, 2008). "In play, and in particular in the diversity of play modes, we learn without at the time knowing we learn," stated Ardley (1967, p. 237). This would appear to be the potential benefit of not only process learning but learning through play.

Transmission style education does not hold much potential for play or even the spirit of play in the classroom. Longo (2010) described the cost to society in terms of instruction delivery methods. Longo argued that "spoon feeding" information to students in hopes of higher tests scores does nothing in the way of generating thoughtful connections between the material and real world applications. Without the opportunity for students to learn to create, connect, and engage, teaching-to-the-test only serves as a temporary fix with the potential for real world deficits when the students graduate (Longo, 2010). Similarly, Kearney (2010) argued against what she described as conditioning. Conditioning is not educating (Kearney, 2010). Educators in the Western culture that fixate on the utilitarian function of education fail to see the long-term benefits of creative and deep learning (Kearney, 2010). Kearney went as far as to note that the long-term goal of education should be to produce creative, happy, spiritually conscious individuals. With all of the arguments in favor of play, I find the increased decline in play (particularly in education) disturbing.

Effects of Play Deprivation

While still under investigated, play deprivation has become a serious theoretical discussion between many fields (i.e., psychology, neuroscience, and education). Worries over the decline in play prompted the founding of the International Play Association in 1961 whose mission includes protecting, preserving, and promoting play (Wenner, 2009). In 1989, the United Nations (UN) ratified the UN Convention on the Rights of Play, which protects children's' right to play around the world ("UN Convention on the rights of the child," 2005). In playing, children learn to make sense of their world and gain the skills and attitudes they will need to function as successful adults (Gray, 2011). Unfortunately, the discussion on the necessity and importance of play for children gets left outside of the classroom (Gray, 2011; Lauer, 2011; Pellegrini, 2009; Sandseter & Kennair, 2011; Wiener, 1999).

Csikszentmihalyi (2000) noted that while many scholars argue for the benefits of play, a difficulty arises in scientifically substantiating the claim because to do so would mean investigating an animal that does not play. Additionally, Csikszentmihalyi noted that, in order to verify benefits, the lack or deprivation of an activity needed investigation. While imperfect, Csikszentmihalyi argued that, at least with human subjects, researchers, looking to determine the effects of not playing, could explain to the subjects that they should function normally with the exclusion of playful activities or those activities not instrumental to everyday life. Non-instrumental activities (e.g., daydreaming, socializing, and watching television) provide intrinsic rewards such as enjoyment. Instead of investigating play deprivation, Csikszentmihalyi investigated a different form of play-like deprivation to determine the effects on humans when they are unable to perform autotelic (self-rewarding) activities over a span of 48 hours. Csikszentmihalyi noted similarities of autotelic deprivation (even in a 48-hour period) to experiences of acute schizophrenics or others with pathological states.

Csikszentmihalyi (2000) described many potential negatives that a lack of enjoyment might have on humans. Using Csikszentmihalyi's analysis of the deprivation study, the multilevel, albeit system-wide, effects depriving students of play-like activities in school could have culture damaging consequences that far exceed simply student boredom and anxiety. Both boredom and anxiety would appear to be the proverbial "tip of the iceberg" in regard to education. Just as learning and motivation self-perpetuate, a negative cycle could also exist. Although Csikszentmihalyi argued that the findings from the deprivation study might be not generalizable or transferable, the potential for similar effects of play deprivation exists for students. Csikszentmihalyi noted that when deprived of play-like activities the participants' ability to think creatively severely declined.

So what motivates, inspires, or even keeps kids in school if it isn't fun? Or better, how can we as educational stakeholders help young people to find what motivates them and rewards them intrinsically and further foster that? These questions led me to the theory of flow as coined by Csikszentmihalyi (1991). In the next chapter, I will attempt to present the theory of flow and describe how it has been studied and how it relates to improv.

Chapter Four

What Is Flow?

"It is almost an out-of-body experience. You are in the moment, and the moment is great. You're able to guide it, but you kinda let yourself go in the scene. And that's when improv's probably the best"
—Briscoe (pseudonym, study participant)

The third conceptual strand on which I based my research was the concept or theory of *flow*. Research links activities such as play and art activities to the state of flow. In this section, I provide a definition of flow, review the literature that connected flow to this study and education, and explain why I believed improvisation held the potential as a flow activity. Because flow activities exemplify self-rewarding activities, learning to find flow in everyday life could be the secret to lifelong happiness (Csikszentmihalyi, 1991).

FLOW AND EDUCATION

Csikszentmihalyi (1991) identified flow as a dynamic state of being during which individuals focus inward while still being part of the activity and their surroundings at large. The result is an optimal state of enjoyment. The state of flow is dynamic. During flow, challenge matches skill, too little challenge results in boredom too much challenge results in anxiety (Csikszentmihalyi, 1991). Researchers have sometimes called flow, *active Zen* (Csikszentmihalyi, 1991). Although flow experiences can differ greatly from person to person, the results of flow experiences always provide the intrinsic reward of enjoyment (Csikszentmihalyi, 1991). Csikszentmihalyi used the Greek word *autotelic* to describe self-rewarding activities in which the reward comes from doing the activity. People perform *exotelic* activities for the extrinsic rewards that follow the activity, such as material gains or benefits (Csikszentmihalyi, 1991). Sometimes people do an activity that is both exotelic and autotelic. Since the formation of the flow theory, researchers have investigated flow in many different fields and disciplines (e.g., Ainley, Enger, & Kennedy, 2008; Bakker, 2005; Csikszentmihalyi & LeFevre, 1989; Dietrich, 2004). Although not current to within 5 years of this book's writing, these studies are included in this book as the authors showed what research and scholarly discussion has happened in the field since Csikszentmihalyi identified flow. Csikszentmihalyi (1991) argued that the human goal of life is happiness. While humans do not experience happiness during moments of flow, the happiness that follows propels and sustains people through the adversity and drudgery of their lives (Csikszentmihalyi, 1991).

The Goal of Education

As I went through school, I never questioned the purpose or goal of education. I always assumed someone higher up, perhaps my parents, saw it as my job. As my own children started to progress through school, I began to question the goal of a traditional education. The more informed I became the less I believed in educating for the American Dream of a high paying job and a house. Instead, I started thinking as others (i.e., Godin, Senge, and Gatto) thought about education. The goal of education should be to create happy, socially competent, young adults who are prepared to take their places in society. Csikszentmihalyi (1991) described the flow theory in terms that have influenced and can influence education by making schools more conducive to flow. With ideas for educational reform, the goal of education should switch to be training for real life experience, life-long learning, and a pursuit of happiness (Csikszentmihalyi, 1991).

Flow in Arts Education

While flow occurs in that sweet spot of an activity where skill matches the challenge, perhaps the most frequent occurrences happen in play activities. In fact, Csikszentmihalyi (1991) noted that play is a quintessential example of a flow activity. Furthermore, Csikszentmihalyi and others have made the connection between art and play, thus connecting flow and art. In a school environment, the potential for giftedness exists in all students, but without the resources or opportunities to discover and nurture talent, they could go unrealized (Csikszentmihalyi, 1991). Ardley (1967) noted that a dichotomy existed in the 1960s that still exists today: schools include either serious studies or ones considered playful. As political policymakers try to achieve higher ranking for U.S. public schools, nonessential instruction (arts and sports) have been reduced or eliminated (Csikszentmihalyi, 1997; A. Johnson, 2004; J. Johnson, 2010). To my surprise, I recently discovered that the arts had been included into the U.S. national standards in 1990s as one of the voluntary core subjects under the then secretary of education, Richard W. Riley (Manegold, 1994). However, due to the fact that states control their educational policies many state policies makers have chosen not to include them.

PRIOR RESEARCH ON FLOW AND EDUCATION

Reviewing the concept of flow, people experience the greatest intrinsic rewards when their skills match the challenges presented to them (Csikszentmihalyi, 1991). When this condition occurs, people have the greatest likelihood to not only enjoy themselves but also stretch their capabilities and build their self-confidence (Csikszentmihalyi & LeFevre, 1989). In this way, people process, change, and report higher overall levels of satisfaction (Csikszentmihalyi & LaFevre, 1989). Although Csikszentmihalyi (1997) alluded to potential beneficial factors (leadership, creativity, and motivation) that relate to flow, no researchers have conducted studies to explore the influence flow experiences have on the development of emerging adults. In the field of education, researchers seek to uncover the elusive nature of ideas such as motivation and engagement in schools. Following the concept of flow, where skill and challenge match, I reviewed the current and seminal research of flow to education. In one such seminal study, Csikszentmihalyi and LeFevre (1989) described flow from the field of leisure research. This idea ties back to the ancient Greek and Roman philosophy of education being a method to pursue leisure studies where leisure provides the greatest source of life rewarding experiences (Csikszentmihalyi & LeFevre, 1989; Huizinga, 1950) and adds positive support to serious play in education at all age levels.

Flow for Students

In recent years, the higher levels of apathy and disengagement in education correlate with school dropout (Ainley et al., 2008; Schmidt, 2010; Senge, 2012; D. Shernoff, 2010; D. Shernoff, Csikszentmihalyi, Shneider, & E. Shernoff, 2003). To investigate this phenomenon, D. Shernoff et al. (2003) performed a quantitative study in which they investigated how students spent their time in high school and under which conditions they reported engagement with the curriculum. While the researchers reported many limitations (i.e., students self-reporting, discrepancies between those who reported and those who did not, and failure to take into account teacher development levels), D. Shernoff et al. reported that the potential for flow in students to be greatest when the classroom activities foster positive emotions and are challenging and relevant to the students. Of interest, D. Shernoff et al. not only described transmission instruction as not conducive to flow, but also an instructional method slow to change. In 2016, this observation holds true, and transmission instruction is used in many classrooms (particularly in higher education) across the country (Sawyer, 2004; Senge, 2012).

D. Shernoff et al. (2003) noted that while teaching strategies, such as collaborative learning, offer a high level of engagement and potential for flow experiences, participants in their study reported experiencing flow during individual classroom work. Csikszentmihalyi (1991) noted that flow could happen individually or in groups, but the intrinsic reward is self-actualized. To answer the question of which flow experience is better, alone or with others, Walker (2010) performed a three-part quantitative study. With respect to education, I stress the importance of Walker's study in that generally students learn in groups. Walker (2010) termed flow experienced in a group of people as social flow. With the findings from the study, Walker supported the hypothesis that operating as a team enhanced the joy the participants felt through flow. I see this information as relevant to education, but also to theatrical improvisers in educational environments who practice and perform as a team.

Flow for Educators

The question of whether or not people experience more joy from individual flow or social flow could be included in the serious play paradox discussion. Classes or groups where many members experience flow could provide greater motivation and engagement. As a social atom, classrooms work together for both teacher and students (Moreno, 2008). However, as described in the literature, transmission instruction with educator-led learning exists in most classrooms (DeZutter, 2008). Bakker (2005) studied potential crossover effects of music teachers' flow experiences and flow experiences of their students. Bakker sought to answer the research question: if music teachers in a Dutch music school experience flow, do their students also experience flow? Answering this question would have added to the knowledge base for social flow and flow in education. However, Bakker (2005) examined variables that described job satisfaction and not flow experiences in the classroom. Bakker underpinned this study on emotional contagion theory and suspected that flow could be contagious. However, Bakker reported data that described flow outside the classroom and not as it occurred within a single experience. The inclusive report still leaves a gap in the knowledge base as to what influence members of a group with different levels of involvement have over the flow experiences of the other members. Future research in this area would determine the amount, if any, of influence educators' flow experiences have in relation to student flow experiences. Research on social flow will also add to the general knowledge base of enjoyment in school and, therefore, possible positive benefits of increased engagement and motivation.

Flow and Extracurricular Activities

Some of the literature presented studies that investigated arts education within the curriculum (Goldstein & Winner, 2012); however, the majority of arts education has been pushed to extracurricular or entirely out of school and into community based programs (Stevenson, Limon, & Reclosado, n.d.). A growing movement exists that argues for the benefits of extracurricular activities as part of a well-rounded or complete education (Senge, 2012). Foubert and Urbanski (2006) showed that participation in clubs and organizations had a positive influence on the development of prosocial skills. Furthermore, higher education staff tended to valorize those students who participated in leadership roles (Foubert & Urbanski, 2006). Although the researchers performed this study many years ago, researchers and educational stakeholders current to the writing of this book use the measure that Foubert and Urbanski (2006) used to evaluate student development (SDTLI) in higher education today, thus adding relevance Foubert and Urbanski's study. Stevenson and Clegg (n.d.) argued that students who participated in extracurricular activities oriented themselves toward their future lives more than those who did not participate in extracurricular activities did. This idea or participation in non-academic activities speaks to the goal of education as being something that prepares students for their future. I argue that academic classes alone do not provide a complete training to prepare young adults for their future.

As of 2010, humans expended close to three trillion hours a year on leisure activities (Ross & Tomlinson, 2010). Before the digital age, many people spent their free time watching television or using their time passively in other ways (McGonigal, 2011; Ross & Tomlinson, 2010). As video gaming grew in popularity, so too did the expenditure of free time playing interactive games and entertainment (McGonigal, 2011). In *Reality is Broken*, McGonigal (2011) argued that many people lack feelings they experience in real life that they experience in game or virtual worlds, making the real world increasingly less attractive and gaming more attractive. Gentile, Lynch, Linder, and Walsh (2004) argued that video games present a problem to society. Contradictorily, Ross and Tomlinson (2010) argued for the strategy of turning tasks into games—*gamifying* leisure time activities to promote social good. Within the context of electronic gaming, Ross and Tomlinson noted limitations for using this cognitive surplus as being wealth and access to technology. However, as noted earlier, in many ways Boal, Moreno, and Fox used psychic or cognitive surplus in the form of applied theatre for decades (Blatner & Wiener, 2007). The significant similarity between the two leisure activities of gaming and improvisational theatre lies in the fun.

This idea brings me back to flow, where optimal enjoyment happens when skills meet challenge. Watching television cannot produce a state of flow the way playing can—it lacks challenge (or frankly skill in general).

While these arguments would seem to advocate for infusing work with the spirit of play or serious play, Csikszentmihalyi and LeFevre (1989) noted social conventions dissuaded people from enjoying their work where the researchers noted the participants reported their greatest number of flow experiences. Csikszentmihalyi and LeFevre conjectured that the lack of flow they observed in their participants' free time indicated that the participants did not know how to organize or optimize leisure. Fostering optimal leisure activities and instructing young adults how to channel their psychic surplus could produce positive social good on the societal level.

Optimizing Leisure for Flow

When speaking of flow, like other scholars, I speak in terms of degrees. People only experience true flow a few times in their lifetime; however, flow like experiences in which people achieve some intrinsic reward can happen several times a day (Csikszentmihalyi, 2000). Teng (2011) posed several hypotheses concerning the traits and characteristics of people who experience some degree of flow. Of particular interest to my study, Teng positively supported the hypotheses that self-directedness negatively related to flow. While self-starters and people who like to work individually can experience flow, higher degrees, and occurrences of flow occur in social or group flow (Teng, 2011; Walker 2010). Nonacademic or extracurricular activities that occur in groups may foster skills that help young adults to be engaged and motivated in whatever endeavors they chose. Although scholars and researchers discussed different aspects of what I have presented in this book, within the scope of my research I could not find any research investigating improv at the college level as an extracurricular activity.

Most of the researchers who have examined flow, play, and improv seem to do so with a mantle of severity. I experienced this with my research. Every time someone asked me about my research I immediately took a defensive position due to the idea that my research lacked importance. Again, I blame a background where science meant only measurable gains or losses and art as something one did as a hobby. Art (or any leisure activity) was extra, as in extracurricular or extraneous. Obviously, I am not the only one to feel that play, art, and leisure activities get a bad rap. In the next chapter, I will expand upon what I see as the paradox of fun.

Chapter Five

The Paradox of Fun

"I think it can change the world. Simply, if all of us were busy doing improvisation, we wouldn't have time for racism and war. So, let's get busy playing."
—Rebecca (Applied Improvisation Professional)

LEGITIMIZING PLAY

So after all the research, all the theoretical work, and even the discourses by Greek philosophers on the benefits of play and art as play to people's well-being, today most educational institutions focus on their curricula on the serious study of science, technology, engineering, and math. It is my hope that by calling improv, *serious fun,* that I have raised improv's level of integrity a tiny bit or at least opened the door to the possibility of acceptance. Furthermore, I argue that having fun is extremely important and that the art of improvisation should be held in reverence and not scorned.

To understand the juxtaposition of the two words—serious play—each word needs consideration on its own. As with improv, playing exists under certain rules or conditions. Play scholars argued that for play to happen it must be voluntary, not real, unconnected with a material interest, timeless in nature, and fun (Brown, 2010; Caillois, 1958; Huizinga, 1950). Huizinga described that any activity could have the spirit of play without totally conforming to all the rules of play. Statler, Heracleous, and Jacobs (2011) described the intentional practice of play for purpose as *serious play.* Using the play spectrum as defined by Caillois (1958) to comprehend play, makes the concept of serious play easier to understand. At one end of the spectrum lies free play, or *paidia,* at the other end structured play, or *ludus.* Placing activities with the spirit of play on the play continuum toward the *ludus* end, best describes serious play. Some play scholars would argue that play can be serious, but not all activities called serious play constitutes play (Brown, 2010).

Play scholars, philosophers, and scientists agree on the importance of play and its features (Burghardt, 2010; Statler et al., 2011). Disagreement lies in the value and understanding of play and education held by educational stakeholders (Burghardt, 2010; Miller, 2010). Some say the opposite of play is work (Burghardt, 2010). Others (Brown, 2010; Sutton-Smith, 2001) argued that the opposite of play is not work but *not play*. Following the logic held by most educational stakeholders, students should play outside of school and should work in school on serious studies. Again, contrary to this idea, school is not children's work (Bodrova & Leong, 2003; Gray, 2013). Furthermore, no reason exists why education has to lack fun.

The paradox comes in making an activity fun. Is this possible? Under the rules that describe play one of the tenets is that the activity has to be voluntary that people need to come to play of their own free will. Back to my imaginary game of tag that I used to describe adherence to rules—how much fun would the game be if it were mandatory? Within the context of education, in particular a mandatory education, I believe educational stakeholders need to figure out a way for students to have more choice and more say in their education, thus opening the door for the potential for fun. Fun then becomes the motivator that propels learning and growth. The study in this book exemplifies this idea through the theme of The Hook, which I describe in Chapter 8. In the theatre, when someone gives someone the hook, it means pulls them off the stage usually because the performance was in some way dreadful. Instead, in this study, I used the term in reference to fishing. Perhaps, I should have used *bait*, because I intended to describe what brought the participants to the extracurricular improv group. However, and more importantly, I wished to describe what they felt caught their fancy and thus "hooked" them on improv. As I describe in the next section, the group I examined met outside of classes and came on their own time of their own free will. In this manner, fun was the gateway to the development the participants reported. Further research is indicated to investigate whether fun within a mandatory curriculum can also promote learning and development.

In Part One, I presented the three strands of the conceptual framework for the study and provided some insight on the relevance of the three strands. Prior research tended to focus on the concepts in pairs. My research bridged a gap joining all three through the perspective of the students. Part Two of the book is an overview of the study.

II

The Study:
The Shared Experiences of
College Improvisers

Chapter Six

Literature Review of
Related Qualitative Studies

In Part One, I offered the origins of the study and presented the three conceptual strands, which I wove throughout the research. In Part Two, I present the
meat of my study. In Chapter 6, I review the related qualitative research
literature in justification for my choice of methodology. In Chapter 7, I
provide an overview of the study. I conclude Part Two by presenting the
themes that emerged from the data.

QUALITATIVE APPROACHES

While researchers from the literature who investigated flow tended to use
quantitative approaches, those researchers who studied group dynamics
(theatrical improvisation) used qualitative approaches (DeZutter, 2008;
Myer, 2006; Sawyer, 2003). Using a reliable measure allowed quantitative
researchers to investigate phenomenon statically and quantifiably. Because
both flow and improvisation happen dynamically and can be interrupted
(Csikszentmihalyi, 1991), reflections on the experience as data would appear
to be strengths of this approach.

Although other researchers who performed various case studies cited in
this review described the inherent value of improvisation to the development
of social and cognitive capacities, scarce few investigated theatrical improvisation as a lived experience. Art and the personal experience of creating it
and viewing it defy the removal of the person from the reporting of the
experience. As seen in qualitative studies (DeZutter, 2008; Lobman, 2003;
Nigh, 2013; Stevenson, 2011), anecdotal reports of experiences in make-

believe worlds can provide insights into the phenomenon of value that statistical reporting could not.

Action Research

Sanguinetti et al. (2005) and Koukounaras-Liagis (2011) approached their investigation through action research in hopes of influencing future practice of adult educators. Miles et al. (2014) described action research as studies in which researchers and participants work together in the investigative process. Sanguinetti et al. (2005) investigated the pedagogy of generic skills for adults. As part of the discussion on the goals and purpose of education, Sanguinetti et al. argued that no difference exists between child pedagogy and adult pedagogy. Sanguinetti et al. described pedagogy as a process involving a dynamic between teachers and students and between students and the relationship to the material and social context. Using this definition and the data from the participants, the researchers, who were also the participants, suggested that pedagogy in any context involves more than teacher-initiated instruction; moreover, learning of generic skill depends on the dynamic nature of pedagogy (Sanguinetti et al. 2005). The researchers constructed the definition based on prior theory; the creation of this definition added to the scholarly knowledge of pedagogy and is a strength of the study. A weakness of this study lies in the research approach and the ethical considerations that the researchers/participants benefit in some way that may unduly influence the outcome of the study.

In a similar manner, because of the action research approach, Koukounaras-Liagis (2011) presented arguments in support of employing TiE as an educational strategy to influence students' perception of cultural diversity. Although the goal of action research appears legitimate, Hammersley (2002) argued that combining the two factors of action research (research and political or social action) poses a threat to either the inquiry or the action that true isomorphism cannot exist between the two factors. Thus, Koukounaras-Liagis offered strong support for inclusion of theatre arts programs as a means for social education; however, the findings from the study represent an editorial stance rather than an empirical one.

Case Studies

Sawyer and DeZutter (2008) examined the group dynamics of DeZutter's afterschool theatrical improvisation group. The group consisted of 13 students age 11–17. While an ethical concern over the relationship of participants and the researcher weakened the study, having Sawyer, who is considered a pioneer in the field of theatrical improvisation research (Myer, 2006), strengthened the reliability of the study. Sawyer and DeZutter argued that to study theatrical improvisation, they needed to focus on observable interactions rather than more traditional data collection such as interviews. Data collection in the form of interviews would have given the researchers an incomplete picture. Sawyer and DeZutter video recorded performances and rehearsals and used interaction analysis, which included using the computer assisted qualitative data analysis software (CAQDAS), Transana. Sawyer and DeZutter identified two types of dramatic structure that the participants cocreated. Of relevance to my study, Sawyer and DeZutter reported on the collaborative emergence that can happen in afterschool adolescent, theatrical improvisation group.

Magerko et al. (2009) also studied theatrical improvisation using a case study approach. Using arguments similar to those presented by Sawyer and DeZutter (2008), Magerko et al. collected data through video recordings and analyzed these data using the CAQDAS, Anvil. Magerko et al. performed what they termed *reflective analysis* through which the participants ($n = 7$), who were professional theatrical improvisers with varying levels of expertise, worked with the researchers reviewing the recordings and analyzing data. The researchers noted a limitation to this analysis as the action of reflection itself, but argued that cognitive instruments employed during the improvisation would have invasively stopped the activity. Magerko et al. argued that theatrical improvisers inherently self-reflect as part of their art work. Although I considered using this type of data collection and analysis, I agreed with Magerko et al. who noted that they sought to understand the action of improvisation; instead, I gleaned meaning from the improvisers' experiences.

Stevenson and Clegg (2011) added to the knowledge base of what value college students in the United Kingdom give to the extracurricular activities in which they participated, and how the subjects ($n = 61$) derived from a larger purposive sample ($n = 640$) felt this participation might influence their future lives. The information Stevenson and Clegg reported represented a large diverse demographic of college students; however, the extracurricular activities varied between students, and the researchers made no distinction between the various types of extracurricular activities (work, art, or athletic). In comparison, Reilly (2009) studied two high school aged males who participated in extracurricular activities (community service and competitive gaming) to determine whether and how the extracurricular activities influenced the participants' intentions for life choices. In both of these case studies (Reilly, 2009; Stevenson & Clegg, 2011), the participants reported rationales for doing extracurricular activities as challenging, motivating, community building, fun, and future orienting. Stevenson and Clegg presented the idea of temporality, which Reilly did not. Some participants reported doing an extracurricular activity as potentially benefitting them in the future; other reported doing the extracurricular activity for the intrinsic rewards they experienced at the time of the activity. The two participants in the Reilly study reported similarly. With the diversity of the activities, it would be interesting to see if one type of activity promoted a specific temporality or rationale for participating in a specific extracurricular activity. A present temporality based on intrinsic rewards could be an indicator of flow.

Older case studies (Lobman, 2003; Miner et al., 2001) added to the bigger picture of the study of improvisation; moreover, they marked the decline of investigation in this field of study. Current research on improvisation tends more toward music education (Koutsoupidou & Hargreaves, 2009) and artificial intelligence design (Magerko et al., 2009). Methodologically, the case study approaches aligned with the researchers' questions but did not influence the design of my study because the researchers investigated specific cases that did not inform my study.

From the current literature, two researchers (Joos, 2012; Stevenson, 2011) performed qualitative studies (grounded theory and ethnography, respectively). Joos noted the negative perception Western culture holds for improvisation. Because of the lack of planning in improvisation, often, pragmatic rational thinkers hesitate to leave future outcomes to chance. This negative perception of improvisation echoes what Caillois (1958) noted about *alea* and the place the element of chance holds for a culture. Joos used action theory to ground his investigation of theatrical improvisation. Although scholars of action theory research argued for a step-by-step process to explain action (Joos, 2012), Joos presented evidence that theatrical improvisers act with a moment to moment flow-like dynamic that could be advantageous to social development and goals. Through observation and analysis, Joos reported that improvisers employ several modes of action. Furthermore, Joos argued for future researchers to interview improvisers to supply data from the participants' point of view, which was the intent of my study.

Stevenson (2011) ethnographically studied an afterschool youth performing arts company in California to determine if youth arts could serve as a catalyst for social change. Although Stevenson reported that participants ($n =$ 18) experienced not only social but also personal change as influenced by their participation in the company, the findings may not be generalizable because the sampled performing arts group focused on social issues. A performance group without such a focus might not attain the same results. To gain insight on whether improvisers without a social change goal focus experience similar outcomes as Stevenson's participants, I examined an improvisation group that only focused on improvisation for entertainment.

Phenomenological Studies

Although researchers who performed case studies, ethnographies, and grounded theory research extended the knowledge in specific areas, the approaches taken still lack the perspective I sought on the shared lived experience. Phenomenological studies provide information about the experiences from the inside (van Manen, 1990). Five of the researchers (Burnard, 2002; Myer, 2006; Nigh, 2013; Treff, 2008; Tuisku, 2010) from the reviewed literature, who performed a phenomenology study, investigated, either tangentially or directly, theatre arts training or improvisation. Of least relevance to my study, Treff investigated graduate students' perceptions of participation training. In the training program, Treff noted the students learned through improvisational theatre and role playing. Treff found the participants reported increased confidence and self-reflective ability. Similarly, the participants ($n = 18$) in Burnard's (2002) study, a musical improvisation group, described value to the collective creativity that occurred during improvisation and an increase in confidence in their ability to interact and perform. Both of these studies (Burnard, 2002; Treff, 2008) occurred more than 5 years from the writing of this book, but the voices of the participants still resonate today in terms of the potential educational value improvisation has for all ages.

Nigh (2013) and Tuisku (2010) performed phenomenological studies with theatre arts students: Nigh in Canada, Tuisku in Finland. While neither of these researchers examined improvisation directly, both underpinned their studies on the theory that theatre arts education provides collaborative learning environments, which when incorporated as Nigh and Tuisku observed, could potentially change educational practice (Nigh, 2013; Tuisku, 2010). With data triangulation, member checks, and third party review, Nigh and Tuisku guarded against threats to validity. Through a phenomenological investigation, Nigh and Tuisku had participants aid in the meaning making of the experiences.

Meyer (2006) performed a phenomenological study, which closely resembled my study. In answering the research question, "What do adult learners experience learning improvisation?" Meyer studied adult learners of theatrical improvisation ($N = 9$) who, except for the researcher who included herself as a participant, had no prior training. Meyer filled a gap in the literature by addressing adult learners and educational engagement and social competency described by improvisers as observed in previous research with younger students. Meyer used a five-part reflective strategy for analyzing data. Furthermore, Meyer argued that the participants of the study were coresearchers who invested in making meaning of their experiences with Meyer. The researcher drew upon three concepts as the framework for the study: (a) organizational improvisation, (b) theatrical improvisation, and (c) adult experiential learning. Although I used some of these concepts I have addressed in reviewing the literature, I widened the scope to include the concepts play and flow. With the current study, the participants belonged to an extracurricular activity, not a class as in the Meyer study, and most had prior training in theatrical improvisation. I hope to extend the knowledge beyond training of theatrical improvisation to its practice and lend insight on how college students make meaning of their development through improvisation.

Chapter Seven

Examining the Shared Improvisation Experiences

"People become sharper by doing improv. What it does is build creativity and helps people see the relationship between two seemingly unrelated things. That is what creativity is really-- seeing things in a different way and seeing the connection between unrelated things."

–Fox (pseudonym, study participant)

METHODOLOGY

"How have experiences with theatrical improvisation training, practice, and performance helped college students make meaning of their ongoing development?"

This was the research question that drove my study. To answer this question, I chose a phenomenological approach in that I wished to examine the shared experiences of these students. Within the vast types of not only qualitative approaches but also phenomenological approaches, I took as heuristic approach as described by van Manen (1990) along with a reflective lifeworld approach as described by Dahlberg, Dahlberg, and Nyström (2008). A large influence on my study came from Dr. Chang (2010) who performed a phenomenological study as his doctoral dissertation and described his experience with it as both "a work of the heart" and "inherently messy" (p. 29). I found these two things to be true of my own study. Many traditional phenomenologists argue for the researcher to remove themselves or "bracket" their knowledge and experiences to remain as objective as possible with the research. This bothered me on many levels in that I felt my prior knowledge and experiences are part of who I am and that I could never completely remove myself from the research. Instead, I took a bridling approach in which I allowed myself to be open and responsive to the research while letting my experiences point me in the right direction. In horseback riding, there is an expression where you let the horse have its head. This means loosening up on the reins to let the horse have some control. For me bridling became a loosening of controlling grip on my research allowing my experiences and knowledge to guide me through my research. I have deep feeling towards improv and what I feel I have gained from my experiences. This was work of my heart. By letting the participants reflect and evolve through the relating of their experiences, I experienced the messiness of which Chang spoke. The interview sessions became individualized very quickly, and my hopes at arriving at a clear picture of the phenomenon of their improv experiences became more difficult. Still, I valued every minute and every statement the participant shared with me. I hope that I have put their thoughts together in way that makes them feel as valued as they are to me.

THE STUDY SETTING

The research setting was a community college in an urban region of the mid-Atlantic region of the United States hereafter referred to as *the college*. Like most community colleges, the college offers certificates, associate degrees, and letters of recognition, continuing education, and extracurricular activities. This college allows not only students in the extracurricular programs but also community members. The college holds as its mission that learning is central. Its philosophy is that students have the time, resources, and opportunities to develop their interests, discover their talents, and foster their potential for a satisfying, stimulating engagement with society. To aid in this mission and philosophy, the department of student engagement lends its own mission to foster engagement in and outside of the classroom. Furthermore, the department of student affairs provides learning opportunities outside the classroom. The department of student engagement aids in the college philosophy that fosters well-rounded individuals engaged not only at the college but also in society. At the time of data collection, the seven participants attended or had attended the college as students. However, while one participant, Fox (pseudonym) met the criteria of having attended the college, during his time of enrollment, no improvisation group existed. In keeping with the research question and focusing on perceived development during college years, data collected from Fox were only included when current student participants noted an experience that included Fox. For this book, I have added Fox's data and my insights on the data into Chapter 10 because, while not applicable to the study, the data was applicable to the larger conversation of improvisation.

The theatrical improvisation group, The Society (pseudonym), falls under the student engagement department of the college. The Society is one of many student-organized groups offered by the college. The college provides the groups meeting space and aids with organizational activities (e.g., planning meetings, recruitment, and budgets). The Society elects two officers each year whose responsibilities include interfacing with the student engagement department and attending monthly meetings. In addition, each group is required to have a staff sponsor who provides oversight for the club's activities. The Society has existed in different forms for approximately 6 years. Originally, one participant, Donnie (pseudonym), founded an improvisation group as part of the theatre department under a different name. This group dissolved after Donnie graduated. Another participant reformed The Society, as the group exists to date.

MEET THE PARTICIPANTS

The Society is open to students, alumni, and community members. The participants reported having as many as 20 members in the group over the past few years and as few as four. The club has had different organizational structures over the years, and as a club was experiencing organizational difficulties due to varying levels of training and the desire to perform during the data collection period. While the group is not exclusive, the senior members felt that a certain level of training and experience with the craft is required for performance. I was unaware of these sentiments when I created my sample criteria. As the sample criteria for the study, volunteers needed to have been with the group for a semester, be or have been students at the college, and performed with the group. All of the participants confirmed that they met the criteria. From the group, seven members volunteered to take part in the study. Table 7.1 shows the demographics and participant characteristics pertinent to this study. At the time of the study, no female members existed in the group. All the participants identified themselves as Caucasian males. The participants range in age from 20 to 29 with the exception of Fox. Two of the participants were current students in associate's degree programs. Three of the participants graduated with associate's degrees. Two participants attended some classes but did not complete any degree or certification program at the college.

Fox was the first participant interviewed. Although he is an alumnus of the college, when he attended, no improvisational group existed. As a member of the community, Fox saw a notice for The Society on a local improv listserv and joined the group in the Fall 2014 semester. Fox trained in a Midwest metropolitan improvisation school with theatrical improvisation legends. Fox described his age as "really old." At the time of data collection,

Table 7.1.   Participant Characteristics and Demographics

Pseudonym	Gender	Age	Years with group	Relationship to college	Years since leaving college as student	Prior training
Flynn	Male	20	2	Current Associate degree student	n/a	High school
Freddy	Male	23	5	Current Associate degree student	n/a	No
Briscoe	Male	23	5 or 6	Alumnus Associate degree	.5	High school
Caine	Male	23	5	Alumnus Associate degree	2	High school
Donnie	Male	29	4	Alumnus Associate degree	9	No
Lester	Male	24	6	Alumnus some classes	2	High School
Fox	Male	"really old"	One semester	Alumnus some classes/member of community	No answer	Midwest Improv school

he practiced and performed with the group regularly. Again, although Fox met the sample criteria, information he provided was only used in the study where I determined his experiences fit the phenomenon of development during college life of others in the study.

Following is the background information for the remaining six participants. Pseudonyms were used for all participants. At the time of data collection:

- Flynn was 20 years old, was pursing an associate's degree in design at the college, and was first exposed to improvisation in high school where another member of The Society sometimes taught improvisation;
- Lester was 24 years old; had joined The Society in 2009, graduated from the college with an associate's degree, and had some prior training in high school;
- Briscoe was a 23-year-old alumnus, graduated from the college with an associate' degree, and had prior training in high school;
- Freddy was 23 years old, a current student seeking an associate's degree from the college, and only trained with The Society;
- Caine was 23 years old, graduated from the college with an associate's degree in transfer studies with a focus in biology, and had first experienced improvisation in high school but was not part of the high school performance team; and
- Donnie was 29 years old, had founded the first improvisation group at the college while taking theatre classes, described himself as self-taught initially with no prior training or experience, and did not graduate from the

college but pursued an acting career and additional theatre training at another university.

The participants reported some of the characteristics and demographics (e.g., prior training, years with the group and relationship to college) in their initial interviews. They were further questioned about these characteristics during the following sessions. Other demographics (e.g., age and race) were obtained later in the data collection process and served as reference points for reflection and areas for organizational development.

DATA COLLECTION

Data was collected in the form of two individual interviews with each participant and a focus group of all the participants. These sessions were recorded, and those recordings were then transcribed. Throughout the collection and analysis process, I was in contact with all the participants and would provide them with the transcriptions and my interpretations to confirm that I had represented them as they wished. The interview sessions and focus group while outlined were not scripted. Instead, I posed this statement to each participant:

Tell me as much as possible about your experiences with improv here at the college, such as practices, performances, or anything that comes to mind.

I was met with a great deal of silence at first. It was a broad question meant as a wide net to catch whatever thoughts the participants had. Appendix A shows the interview protocols I used to inform my data collection sessions. Because I did not ask the same questions in the same order of every participant, I note this as a limit to the study but justify doing it this way as a means of probing the participants' memories in a bridled manner following my own instincts.

I thoroughly enjoyed all the interview sessions. It was satisfying to watch each participant make connections and to share their art with me. However, it was the focus group session that was the most transformative for me. I did not anticipate the data, the reactions, or the manner in which they presented the data. In response to asking them to speak one at a time for transcribing purposes, the participants came up with the idea of using a pair of socks as "talking socks" —whoever held the socks could speak. The tone of the focus group was passionate, reverent, and with a spirit of play as they passed the talking socks back and forth expressing ideas of art versus craft, group mindedness, and synergy. Afterwards, nearly every participant mentioned their surprise at how their teammates felt about their experiences. Furthermore, following that session, the participants had a rehearsal for an upcoming show. They also expressed later how they felt it had been their best rehearsal ever. I mention the focus group and the interview sessions not so much to show what I did or how I did it but to lay the groundwork for the themes that emerged from the sessions. The participants in the study evolved, and they took me along for the ride.

In the next chapter, I describe the themes that emerged from the data. In an iterative process, I referred back to the participants with my thoughts as I went along. Together, the participants and I gave shape to their ideas and feelings.

Chapter Eight

The Themes

"My fascination with improv comes really from self-improvement as a performer and as a person. The act of creating something from nothing, with no medium other than yourself, is fascinating to me. It uses a part of your brain that a lot of people don't use…It has helped me in lots of different areas in my life."
—Freddy (pseudonym, study participant)

INTRODUCTION OF THEMES

Restating, the purpose of this phenomenological study was to discover and to describe the lived experience of improvisational acting training, practice, and performance of community college students and alumni who participated in an extracurricular activity improvisation group. I asked students and alumni to describe their experiences joining the group, interacting with the group, their perceptions on their sense of competency with improvisation as influenced by their experiences, and the role their experiences had on their college experiences and ongoing development. Insights into the complex experiences had by theatrical improvisers at a community college campus are necessary to aid stakeholders (i.e., students, faculty, student affairs personnel, and policy makers) in promoting, creating, and implementing a holistic educational program.

Through responses to interview and focus group questions, the participants expressed a variety of ways in which they felt their development had been influenced by their experiences with theatrical improvisation while attending a community college in the mid-Atlantic region of the United States. These responses highlighted the importance of having an active and open venue for theatrical improvisation on future campuses and supportive college organizations, such as student affairs, for student development and community building. Two of the participants were current students. Four of the participants were alumni (three with associate degrees) who choose to return to the college to rejoin the group. One participant had been a student at the college years prior to the existence of the group but returned to the college community to join the improvisation group. While all the participants' descriptions of their experiences varied slightly, saturation of data occurred, and four major themes emerged that addressed the research question.

The participants described a heightened awareness of their development through the reflective nature of the phenomenological approach. All the data was then sorted into codes or similar ideas. I then sorted the codes into themes. The themes that emerged took a semichronological order. The Hook described experiences with what drew the participants to the group and theatrical improvisation. In The Craft, the participants identified skills and qualities required of an improviser. The theme of The Rewards and Application consisted of perceptions by the participants of their use of their identified skills outside of the group. The fourth theme, The Continuance, addressed future ideas on the participants and their relationship to the group, future ideas of the group, and the continued relationship with the college. I chose to present the findings as the aforementioned themes rather than as a descriptive narrative as other phenomenologists sometimes choose to do. While the stories told by the participants in the interviews were full of passion, humor, and insight, I felt the presentation of the results thematically better described the essence of the collective experiences of the participants.

The Hook

Through reporting the results of the first theme, The Hook, I describe how the participants came to be part of the group. Of these data, the information about how the participants began their experiences with The Society proved to be the most distant yet distinct memory for all the participants. As an extracurricular activity, The Society represented an activity and space away from academics and other outside pressures they experienced at the college. Notably, the experiences of joining The Society were more often than not contrasted with negative experiences and perceptions of activities of outside the group (i.e., work, partying, and school). Most of the participants reported that what initially drew them to The Society changed as their experiences with the group progressed.

Prior Experience/exposure

One of the first codes to emerge from collected data concerned prior exposure or experiences with theatrical improvisation. Many of the participants grew up watching the television show, *Whose Line Is It Anyway?* They mentioned it as factoring into their desire to join an improv group. As a rationale for forming the original improvisation group, Donnie stated, "We really wanted to have an improv...like a place we could go and learn about this art of improv, and I had never done it before. I just saw *Whose Line* and really wanted to do it." Freddy remembered being drawn to the group after recognizing a fellow student who was a group member and making the connection to the television show.

> I grew up with the show, *Whose Line Is It Anyway?* I have always been curious about it. I hadn't been exposed to it in any theater groups or anything like improv before where I grew up. I realized that one of the cast members was in one of my classes so I approached him and said, "Hey, I saw the show, and it was great." He said if I enjoyed it, I should come out to the club sometime.

Lester echoed Donnie's and Freddy's remembrances of the television show, "We loved, even as a kid, loved the show, *Whose Line Is It Anyway?* I wanted to be just like them; I thought it was funny." As an outside, older observer, Fox noted that improvisation did not exist while he was at the college. Fox expressed surprise and pleasure at the accessibility of theatrical improvisation at the college today and credited the television show for making improvisation more mainstream. Three other participants (Briscoe, Caine, and Flynn) had learned theatrical improvisation in high school and were looking to reconnect to the art form to improve their improvisational skills and for fun.

Inviting and Inclusive

The Society has no audition process to limit membership. This differs from other improv groups I have experienced before, which often have such an audition process as a gate to joining. Caine reported negative feelings toward improvisation from his high school years. In high school, the group was "competitive," and Caine did not make that team although he auditioned several times. Unlike his high school experiences, Caine's expressed relief and a sense of welcoming from the members of The Society that he now employs with new members of The Society. "We never turn someone down and say, 'You cannot be here.' We welcome everyone." Freddy experienced the same openness to join when the fellow classmate invited him to come to the club after Freddy complimented him.

Friendship

Beyond the openness of the group, strong strands of friendship wove through all of the participants (except Fox) descriptions of the group's appeal. Many of the participants had been friends or knew each other from high school or prior to joining the group. All of the participants reported a sense of friendship with all members of the group. When questioned as to which came first, the friendship or the group, a few of the participants noted the friendship was first, and a few said their friendships evolved from their experiences. Joining the group to be with friends seemed to be less of an attractor and more of what has kept the group going.

Leisure/recreation

Counter to my stereotypical idea of how college-aged men would choose to spend their Friday evenings, the participants described "eagerness," "anticipation," and "can't wait 'til Friday" feelings for meeting to do improvisation. As Flynn stated, "I am just really, really into improv."

As an older member of the group, Lester mentioned the partying aspect of college, and why he preferred his time with the improvisation group. "I feel fulfilled afterwards. I have done the partying thing. It is fun at the time, but you just feel like crap afterwards. But with improv, you can't wait till next Friday."

For all of the participants, their experiences with the group began with feelings of looking for fun and an outlet or escape from other experiences in their lives. As a diversion or a means to laugh, the participants felt their shared experiences rounded out their lives and gave them a place to laugh, play, and bond as have been noted in other leisure and recreational activities. Donnie mentioned he looked forwarded to doing improvisation every Friday and not to anything else that was "not improv."

Fun

The participants described "fun" as the predominant draw to the group mentioned by the participants. Whether they described it as "acting goofy" or "addicted to laughing" or simply "playing," all the participants joined the group in search of fun. Donnie described it as an adult play aspect of improvisation.

> I realized that it's so much more fun for me to play with someone than to play by myself, and I think it's also beyond being human.... I think it's the closest you get to being a kid again.... It's the same process children do . . . it's just that now you understand all the underpinnings of why it works . . . like I don't think it's any different from what we do on stage than what small children do with action figures or when they put on a cape or anything like that.

Outlet

I placed the subcode of outlet in this section; however, while the participants overwhelmingly described the group as such, few mentioned it as what attracted them to the group. Most of the data supported the idea that their experiences became an outlet, an escape, and bordered on therapeutic. Those participants (Briscoe, Flynn, and Caine) with prior improvisational experience did link their attraction to the group with ideas of doing so as an outlet. As part of his inclusive philosophy toward the group, Caine stated:

> It's an outlet. It's therapeutic. It's anything you want to call it whoever is in there. It's different for everyone for their reasons, so if there is someone that just needs that outlet, and they don't have anywhere to go.... We just want them to come to improv, to help them out. It'll help with the troupe; it will help them out.... It's a win, win every situation.

THE CRAFT

In this section, I describe the theme of The Craft that emerged as the participants described their involvement with the art of improvisation. The participants identified many skills, abilities, and qualities that they attributed to their experiences. The ideas between art and art work, process and product, and art and craft are woven throughout this section and are inseparable. The participants described the development of the following attributes through the holistic set of their experiences. While I report specific instances, as identified by the participants, it is the relationship of the instances to the larger picture, which helped the participants make the identifications and connections. I divided this section into three areas to differentiate between skills (which can be learned), abilities (which can be practiced), and qualities (which can be fostered). This is done within the context of the shared experiences of the participants.

Skills

The participants identified these skills as needed to be good at improv. They recognized them in themselves and in other members of the group. The realization of these skills emerged from stories the participants told of memorable scenes or games that they had played. Further recognition and identification of what the participants thought made a good improviser came from the focus group session and reflection between the data collection sessions.

The participants had many terms for experiences, which I coded as presence. For example, the participants described presence as both "focus" and as "in the moment." How much the improvisers committed to or developed this skill led to their feelings of success in their craft. In many instances, the participants noted the realization of having presence as a transformative moment. Freddy described presence as emotional attunement to what happens on stage and tuning out what happens off stage.

> It really happens like an epiphany. It happens to all of us even from the beginning. Our big "Ah, ha!" moments come from performance in and onstage. We just reach this level of awareness, and we're able to build off of it onstage...We get this optimal idea of the beats and what needs to be added. It happens more and more frequently. You get better at it every time you do it, you reach a new checkpoint in your abilities, and you widen sort of this tree branch system of skills whether it is pantomime or leading the scene or listening very carefully and just being able to focus. Focus is really critical and the ability to really almost become meditative...only listening to what's happening on stage and then not paying attention to what's happening in the audience. That's the big key to becoming a good improviser. It's really a school of fish-like understanding of your other improvisers, of your fellow improvisers, rather than just trying to make the laugh.

Freddy described the skill of focusing as something that group members learn early in the training process and that the more they practice, the better they get at it. Flynn described being in the moment as a being in a "purely reactionary state...being emerged in the energy of the people around you." Like Freddy, Flynn argued that being able to get to this "state" (or skill level) took practice. Flynn also noted that failing to achieve presence and that the awareness presence presents were instructive parts of the process of improvisation.

All of the participants reported self-awareness as a predominant skill needed for improvisation. Furthermore, the improvisers touched on different aspects of self-awareness (i.e., emotional, physical, and mental). A couple of the participants reflected on being shy and even scared to get up in front of others and perform. While shyness might appear counter indicative for a performer, the awareness of this aspect of themselves helped them become better at improvisation. Flynn described learning self-awareness as the acceptance of failure. He said the recognition of knowing about himself helped him become a better improviser.

> At first just getting more comfortable failing in front of people, I felt like it can be like really, really scary, really threatening. When you don't have the confidence and you are not 100% sure in your ability to not make the same mistake or to not make other mistakes in the future. I know I had some anxiety when I first started improvising. It could be terrifying when I would like go up (on stage). I'd shut down a little bit and then just go on autopilot. Maybe I would say something or do something, and it wouldn't make any sense. It wouldn't make for a good scene... It would be kind of the exact wrong thing to do, but I've noticed it... when you have people in the scene that help you justify and take that mistake...together you can turn it in into like a strength.

Learning to be self-aware through improvisation was easier for some of the participants because of the nature of the art form. The Society practices and performs short form improvisation; similar to the games and scenes performed on *Whose Line Is It Anyway?* The scenes run only a few minutes, are generally humorous, and when completed the improvisers move on to the next game. Many of the participants noted that it was easier to be vulnerable and learn about their mistakes and successes in this medium. Several of the participants mentioned "laughing off" bad scenes and simply moving on to the next. Laughter and the knowledge that failures are not catastrophic, aid in the process of becoming more self-aware. Freddy described one of his moments of self-awareness during a performance of a game in which the audience voted him to be scene "winner."

> I went through the scene, and I really was carried by adrenaline. But adrenaline wouldn't take you very far in that game because you have to be mindful of everything else that has to happen in the scene. And I hit that, I hit that magic balance of adrenaline and focus of what was going on, what I need to do. It was really the moment that I realized that I had potential in improv and that improv really made me happy because if its developmental qualities.

All the participants described the skill of listening as something they learned through their experiences with improvisation. Donnie said improvisers need to have listening skills:

> The basic skill of improv is listening. I notice that after doing improv I really listen and that I want to hear someone. It makes me pay attention; it helps me stay within the moment. I am not thinking what I am doing an hour from now, or 3 days from now. I am thinking of right now and what's happening.

Donnie addressed the interconnectedness of the skills the participants identified as needed for improvisation. Lester identified listening as one of his strengths.

Freddy added watching, which I included as part of this theme because of the physical and presentational nature of this art form. The participants demonstrated their watching skills during the focus group session. Using the convention of the "talking socks," the participants moved the discussion physically as well as orally. Often a participant would ask for the opportunity to speak through gesture or eye contact. Sometimes a group member directed the conversation by throwing the socks at another member. Had any member not been fully watching or listening throughout the session, the socks would have dropped, been missed, or hit someone. However, this never happened during that session. I was able to observe how the group functioned using skills they had identified in the initial interview session. Again, the three skills identified in this theme represent only ones that the participants reported and are not indicative of all the skills or are the only ones that might be developed through improvisation.

Abilities

The participants reported that while all people may have the capacity to be patient, to trust, and to be creative; through their experiences with The Society, they have practiced these skills and improved them through the process of their craft. All of the participants thought anyone could do theatrical improvisation. They all also recognized areas for improvement in themselves and others to do the art form better. In this subcode, I developed a sense that the participants had an ideal of a good improvisational performer and that abilities (i.e., patience, trust, and creativity) factored into the participants' evaluations of themselves and others.

Most of the participants described early experiences with the group as "adrenaline" or "endorphin" rushes. The key word in these descriptions was "rushes" indicating quickness without thought. Lester argued that although those moments were fun and exhilarating that over time, he learned to wait and listen instead of rushing into a scene or pushing his agenda.

> I used to force myself to be as quick as possible, and I realized how unrealistic it is. Cause in real life, you are silent, you are a listening to people, you are thinking about what I am saying, you're reacting, even a head nod, you are actively listening. That is how people talk, you are not trying to interrupt me, you're registering in your brain. So, I thought about that, I should bring it into improv and make it more real. When it is real, it's more relatable. When it's more relatable, to me, it's funnier.

Patience on the part of the improviser limits the chaos and keeps the scenes moving forward. To be patient, the participants noted that they had to improve their skills of listening and being self-aware.

Similarly to the other skills and abilities, the ability to trust has many layers and implications. The improvisers described the need to trust themselves to have the skills and patience to not only help the scenes but to make them better. After recognizing the ability to trust their own skills, the participants identified trusting their troupe mates as an important ability. In the following statement, Lester gave some insights on trust.

> You definitely have to have trust. This is something that can play on a lot of people insecurities, not just like...not just being able to trust someone in a scene to help you develop the scene, but trust them not to throw you under the bus. It is a team effort to make the scene work, and a lot of times the hardest thing to get over is the need to make sure you have a good joke. You want to be able to trust the person to be flexible, to play to their strengths, but also to try on things that they are not as strong with. Because they know that if they

falter in this regard, you're there to help them. That's the coolest part about it (improv); you're all working together, to make this scene work. It's not just one person's responsibility. So trust is super important.

Donnie described the ability to trust his troupe mates by using a Marine saying, "Welcome to the suck." The idea behind the saying is that no matter how bad the situation might be, the group trusts they will not only get through it together, but the outcome might be better for the challenge. In the focus group, Donnie gave this example: "We actually have a game, *Dr. Hands*, where somebody else is your hands (from behind the person speaking) and usually involves food. During rehearsal, we did this. Freddy shot…was it make-up? He shot something up your (Lester's) nose?"

"It was paint," interjected Lester, laughing.

Donnie continued:

Completely up Lester's nose... that's the most uncomfortable physical game. The other person can't see...the other person is just trying to mess with you. But having to trust no matter what ...if they will kill you?...but then, I think it's more interesting.

The group laughed in acknowledgement and recognition to this remembrance.

While Donnie jokingly mentioned that the scene might "kill you," the group knew and trusted that no one would ever let a situation get that far. The bonds and friendships that the participants described framed their knowledge of their fellow improvisers. The participants described their troupe mates' strengths and weaknesses and how they used them in the scenes. Along with the making friendships comes the ability to trust and, as Briscoe noted, not to be "thrown under the bus."

Similarly to many of the subcodes identified, the participants described the ability of creativity in many different ways (i.e., inventive, innovative, funny, quick thinking, and artful). Briscoe noted that he enjoyed being around others who shared his sense of humor and fun. Lester reported that he needed his Fridays with improvisation as a "creative outlet." All of the participants agreed that everyone has the capacity to be creative, and improvisation not only provided the opportunity to learn creativity but also the outlet to share it. Freddy gave the analogy of muscles; that they need to be flexed and exercised to be effective. Every Friday night, this group of individuals "flexes" their creative muscles in hopes of becoming better at the process of improvisation.

Qualities

The participants identified attributes of a person (i.e. supportive, selfless, and confident), which make them better at improvisation. Furthermore, the participants described that the more improvisational experiences (positive or negative), the greater the positive growth in these qualities, and the better they felt they became at improvisation. The participants recognized these qualities in themselves and in their teammates. The qualities of supportive, selfless, and confident were often described in the same statement and addressed the social nature of this art form.

I mentioned earlier that most of the rules I identified from the literature were not equally identified by the participants in this study. One rule the participants did state frequently was making the other people on stage look good. In the following quote, Donnie described the relationship of selflessness to the art of improvisation:

> You start to forget about you, and it becomes this very selfless art. And it's weird because usually, art is almost by nature selfish...I want to produce something that makes people feel this...or expresses this idea I have, or this is mine, and this is how I feel.... and I feel this (improvisation) is almost different because it's entirely wrapped in being social, and I think your strength as an improviser is so much wrapped up on how well you can communicate with someone.

The improvisers described a delicate balance between challenging their fellow troupe mates and supporting them. In challenging each other, they argued they became more creative and, often, funnier. However, the only way they could challenge each other was to give focus of the scenes over to their fellow actors and support them through the challenge.

"I was super shy," said Lester, "still am a little bit." Lester spoke about his early days with the group when he doubted his abilities at improvisation. He reflected that he took laughter as a measure of his ability. However, as he developed his skills, he felt he no longer needed to "go for the laugh." As one of the younger members of the group, Flynn described himself as shy and lacking self-confidence. While Flynn noted that his experiences in high school helped raised his self-confidence, at the college level, he noted that he felt that he still had room for improvement in this area. Flynn spoke in admiration of some of his troupe mates, who had more experience than he had, and that while he felt confident in his abilities, he also noted that confidence required continual work.

THE REWARDS AND APPLICATIONS

The predominance of life applications connections that emerged from the data was remarkable. While intuitively and experientially I had made the connections for myself, the importance the participants placed on the transferability of theatrical improvisation to life outside the activity surprised me. Donnie said it simply and best in the following statement: "Everything that I ever needed, I learned in improv." Donnie was not alone in this thought. All of the participants reflected on development they attributed to their experiences with improvisation and gave applications for things they learned through their craft to many aspects of their lives.

To Person

Of the skills, qualities, and abilities that the participants identified and I wove into the theme of The Craft, the improvisers described how they felt they had changed or developed personally. Flynn reported that his experiences helped shape who he was as a person. Confidence, Flynn felt as an improviser, influenced how he felt about himself outside of the group.

> The kind of confidence...I didn't know I had... the kind of ability I didn't, I wasn't fully aware of. I guess I just have become a little bit more confident, a little bit more spontaneous as a result of thinking more deeply on this (improvisation).

All of the other participants reported similar experiences (i.e., awareness of confidence, listening skills, and collaboration) and applications to their personal development. Freddy added memory rehabilitation to rewards that he felt he gained from being with the group. Head surgery had damaged Freddy's short-term memory. Freddy remembered practices where he worked on rehabilitating his memory skills. Freddy mentioned how he believed that theatrical improvisation would be helpful to anyone who might be suffering from memory problems (i.e., Alzheimer's disease or dementia) or for "growing brains like students" too. Other members of the troupe also thought that improvisation training would be good for any age.

During the focus group the participants discussed whether they believed their experiences were an outlet or therapeutic. Most of them said it could be both. Because the material for the scenes was unscripted and created spontaneously by the improviser, the participants described how that process could border on therapy. Lester described his experiences as the reward of emotional outlet and a form of therapy:

> I feel like it's definitely an outlet, because if I don't do improv for a week I feel like my brain is congested with all this like creative energy. I need to get it

out, or I'm going to explode and be very upset...(but also) everything we do in
the scene is drawn from like experiences we've had...We know, in that sense,
it's kind of therapeutic because if we have a scene...like a relationship we've
had, we are drawing from what we know. So in that sense it can be therapeutic,
you're making fun of things that you have experienced so it's becoming light-
hearted and hopefully maybe it helps you cope with things better.

Briscoe, Donnie, and Caine also described how they escaped the cares of the
day when they came to improvisation practice. The participants used the
word "addictive" to describe their feelings towards their experiences.

Although none of the participants had heard of Csikszentmihalyi's theory
of flow, all of them described it using different terminology. The feelings of
"being addicted to improv" came when the participants described the feelings
of joy and happiness after what they deemed a successful scene, practice, or
performance. Briscoe stated,

> It is almost an out of body experience. As far as, you are in the moment, and
> the moment is great. And you're able to guide it, but there is this sense that the
> scene has a natural progression not defined. You're able to kinda let yourself
> go in the scene, and that I think when it's probably the best.

They all described how challenging the craft is and how rewarding. Achiev-
ing that balance, those feelings of "the synchronicity," "harmony," and of a
"good scene" kept the participants wanting more.

To Social Life

Donnie noted that many people who have not done improvisation lack the
self-awareness that can develop from improvisation. Donnie identified the
lack of self-awareness as a societal flaw.

> It (improvisation) helps me to actually connect with the other person across
> from me in a not superficial way. Whereas in other times, before I started
> doing this, I felt like I started conversations because I needed something, or I
> just wanted to say something myself. I feel like my conversations are less
> selfish because I feel like I surrender to everything that is happening around
> me more than I have in the past. I think less about me and more of what is
> happening and accepting it for what it is. Because that is what you do as
> improvisers.

Many of the participants conjectured that if more people had the improvisational skills they identified, the world might be a better place.

The friendships that the participants have created while in this group were
described as much more than casual acquaintances that they felt they made
outside of the group. A bond exists between them through their experiences.

Many of the participants described liking their troupe mates and "hanging out" with them outside of practice or performance, but trusting, supporting, and caring for them "like family." Through pushing past what they felt were their faults and vulnerabilities, the participants described making connections that have only strengthened over time.

To School

While attending college and participating in the group, both Caine and Briscoe used their time with the group as motivation. Both recognized that they did not feel that their academics skills were strong and further described some of their academic classes as drudgery. Briscoe used his improvisational skills within the class to make the content "more fun." Caine used improv practice as a reward at the end of the week for going to all of his classes and doing the required work. Lester and Freddy described learning improvisation as being superior to learning public speaking as a means to develop social skills. Lester had taken a public speaking class concurrently to being in the group; the professor of the class excused him from the final examination. Lester attributed that to his improv training and not to what he had learned in the class. All of the participants argued that their experiences helped them make more creative and fun answers to problems in and out of the realm of academia.

THE CONTINUANCE

All seven participants were passionate about the group. Just like their scenes, the future of the group and the role each member holds or will hold are unscripted and changeable. The participants recognized the tenuous existence of the group due to its structure and the relationship with the college. Some of the participants did not know how long they would continue with the group, but were happy to be with it for "the now." All of the participants had ideas on what they felt they needed to keep the group going as it was at the time of the study, and the role theatrical improvisation should have at the college level.

Internal Changes to The Society's Organizational Structure

The participants described the several incarnations of the group over the 9-year period since Donnie first formed an improv group at the college. As a club, the benefits include inclusiveness and non-threatening aura of "goofy fun." However, the participants noted performance as an important factor in this art and further acknowledged a need for training prior to performance. Some participants described this incongruity of openness to everyone yet not everyone having the capacity to perform as being an underlying worry for the group falling apart. One participant described the problem this way:

> Imagine having this kinda thing (a situation where a person requires skill level to perform) for like a football team. Say, anyone can come in and play on the team with you, but you are going to want to develop the people who you have on the team already to make sure that they work better. I do think that is a better way for performance; however, I love the club thing too cause I love being able to bring in people from all over...I think it is cool to get people excited and find an outlet for it and discover it.

The senior members of the group continued to discuss the problem and planned to make changes to the club structure in the future to accommodate a club-like environment, but also, a performance troupe.

Relationship to the College

Two of the participants of this study held leadership roles in accordance with the requirements of having a club at the college. These participants described what they identified were the benefits and downsides of the relationship with the student affairs department at the college. Benefits included weekly, free rehearsal space and several performance dates and spaces over the school year also free. Unlike other clubs at the college, the participants noted that they did not require a budget to operate; the participants felt they required little oversight from the college. However, to maintain their club status, a member of The Society is required to attend a monthly meeting, which the participants reported was difficult to do. General sentiment between all the participants was that the group was well-liked by the college community. After one of their performances, the participants reflected they should have done more advertising as they recognized that performances also attracted new members to the group.

When I asked about The Society's relationship to the theatre department, the participants gave short and negative responses. One improviser said, "They (the theatre department) think we're not an art, and we make fart jokes...and I have heard that exact thing repeatedly that we make bathroom humor, and that's all we are." The theatre department at the college does not teach theatrical improvisation, and several alumni members noted this to be true at the 4-year institutions they transferred to after receiving their associate's degree from the college. All of the participants argued that if not an entire class, at least a portion of an acting class offered at the college should cover theatrical improvisation. The sense that others in theatre regarded the improvisers' art as inferior by others was mentioned in both the interviews and the focus group. Nonetheless, the participants reported the rewards they perceived from their improvisational experiences with pride and passion that belied simply "making fart jokes." Donnie said, "I think people need to view it (improv) as the art, as the beautiful, wonderful, scary, dirty, gross, awesome art that it is."

Validation

Understanding the conflicts, such as organizational challenges and outside perceptions on the art, led to feelings of validation by the participants. In the final interview that followed the focus group, all the participants described how listening to the other members talk about their craft helped them in several ways. Some mentioned that they thought they were the only ones who felt about improvisation and The Society as they did. Some mentioned feeling more connected through their shared passion. Some thought they were the only ones who saw past the humor and goofiness to the seriousness and aesthetics of improvisational theatre. According to Lester,

> It's good that this art form stays alive for people...They can just do it whenever they feel like doing it. You don't need anything. It's free; all you need is a space. You can do improv anywhere. It is good for you developmentally, for your brain. It's good socially. If you have that fear being in front of people, it's good for you. It helps you vent out ideas. It is a great stress reliever; you get to laugh. If you laugh a lot, I heard you live longer, which is good or bad, depending on how you look at it. I think it is good. It's super important; it's super important.

Continued Experiences

All of the participants appreciated the community, club aspect of the group. All the participants commented on the benefits they perceived from Fox's membership to the group. As a community member with prior theatrical improvisation experience, the participants described learning new techniques and scenes only added positively their experiences. Alumni members expressed appreciation in being able to have a place to practice and perform their art. Again, not only is improvisation nonexistent in many colleges, it is restricted to students or even only to theatre students. As long as the members can adhere to the requirements set forth by the college, The Society can continue. What organizational structure The Society takes in the future has yet to be determined. The participants reminisced about members who had moved away, graduated, and left. Often when they did so, they spoke fondly of the former members and gave a sense of missing them. The participants recognized that someday they would no longer be with the group, but that their experiences will be with them forever. For now, come Friday evening at 7 pm, the participants look forward to their creative outlet.

REFLECTIONS

In the methodology section of Chapter 7, I described phenomenological research as both *work of the heart* and *inherently messy* (Chang, 2010). My interconnection to the subject matter of the study as well as my desire to understand other improvisers' perceptions of their experiences made both those aspects of phenomenological research a reality for me. Through the process of bridling my knowledge and experiences, I noticed a change in myself. While I did not think I allowed my experiences and thoughts to enter any aspect of the data collection sessions, they did so in a way I had not anticipated. Instead of coloring or directing the responses, I listened and thought of how to capture the participants' responses in the best possible way. In essence, I practiced good improvisational skills. In that regard, I too adhered to the improvisational rule of making your scene partner look good.

The paradox of wanting to have fun and understanding the importance of their play presented the participants with a desire for validation. After the initial interview, when I gained their trust, the participants eagerly shared with me. Sometimes, long after the recording stopped, the participants shared about thoughts on how to advertise for an upcoming show, future recruitment ideas, or even preferred versions of Dungeons and Dragons. However, during the interviews and focus group proper, the participants focused on the questions related to the research. Following the focus group, the participants described having had "the best practice" because of discussing their experiences as a group. The participants acknowledged that increased reflection and group discussion could only increase the potential for group growth. In the final interview, the participants expressed pleasant surprise of their troupe mates' feelings and thoughts on the group. In the end, the participants extended me an open invitation to join The Society. Whether due to their perceptions of improvisational skills or as one participant said as he walked out the door, "Besides we need girls," I felt I had given them a sense of validation for their serious fun. In Part III, I describe the impacts of this study and extend the findings to the larger community.

III

How Improv Can Change the World

Chapter Nine

Everything I Needed to Learn in Life I Learned from Improv

"I feel like it's good for the development of individuals, and I can be selfish because I feel like I learned so much from it. But I don't see how you can't. I don't think there's a single individual that cannot learn from this and cannot do improv and get better."
—Donnie (pseudonym, study participant)

SOCIAL COMPETENCY

Each day humans of any age face a myriad of decisions. One of the big ideas I am presenting in this book is that learning how to successfully navigate the chaos of life should be a goal of education at any level. The purpose of this book is not to teach you how to improvise. Learning how to improvise from a book seems about as practical as learning how to negotiate nuclear warfare from a book. Sure both can be terrifying, but sometimes you need that experiential element to learn, even if that experience is make-believe. Instead, the purpose of this book is to reinforce the value of play and improvisation as play to a person's overall well-being and success in life. Through improv, actors have an opportunity to try out different decisions in a safe environment. Of the participants in the study, only one pursued a career in theatre. However, all of them valued their experiences and applied them to the rest of their lives as I described in the theme of The Rewards and Applications.

In recapping not only what the participants said but what I gleaned from other improv scholars have said, improv helps people learn how to:

- Listen
- Trust (yourself, others, and the work)
- Be present
- Collaborate and cooperate
- Fail
- Not only share but also think about how to make the other person look better
- Build confidence

I explored the shared experiences of seven collegiate theatrical improvisers as they learned, practiced, and performed in an extracurricular activity improvisation group at a community college. The participating synergy of improvisers included two students enrolled in associate's degree programs, three alumni who graduated with associate's degrees, and two alumni who had taken some classes at the college but not graduated; all of the participants were men. Replication of this study with similar experiences of theatrical improvisation at college but with a more diverse sample population would strengthen the findings of this study and make them more transferrable.

The Society functions as an extracurricular activity under student and alumni governance. The participants provided ideas and rationales for greater inclusion of theatrical improvisational activities in higher education because of their reflection of their own developmental gains. Future researchers could also strengthen the findings of this study by examining other theatrical improvisational groups on different higher education campuses with different organizational structure such as those under the purview of college theatre departments to compare theatrical improvisation experiences with different organizational structures. Findings from research where theatrical improvisation has been experienced in a classroom environment rather than as a club could further add to the understanding of influences of the craft to education. In the following sections, I discuss what I believe lie at the heart of improv making it such a powerful developmental tool.

PLAYING

The participants described playing as the lure of improv. While the spirit of play and elements of fun are important, it is the meeting of the minds, the becoming something new (together) that playing produces. Playing with others provides us with the opportunity to share ourselves in ways that daily interactions do not provide. In a conversation, which a basic form of improv, people may begin as individuals but as each contributes to the conversation adding thoughts, feelings, and imagination, the conversation becomes more than the individual contribution. It takes on a life of its own. There is give and take. Topics and goals grow as a result of the mutual agreement to play together and follow certain rules.

I gave the example of a game of tag earlier in the book to illustrate adherence to rules. There is an improv game called *freeze,* which also helps illustrate the power of improvisational play. While there are many variations of freeze, the basic game starts with two players who begin their scene with a *get* or suggestion from the audience. The *get* is usually a noun from which the players begin. Other improvisers stand to the side or in the back (sometimes called the *backline actors*), not as audience. Improvisers watch with the purpose of supporting the other players and helping the scene and are active watchers. Spolin (1989) called detached, passive watching as *becoming audience.* Within the context of play, this makes sense. If you are playing but not immediately active (e.g., being chased, being it), you still need to be alert and in the game. Back to freeze. After the two initial players have established the scene and made their goals clear, an off stage player yells, "Freeze!" Players on stage instantly freeze, and the caller tags out one of the two players. The freezer assumes the physical position of the person that was tagged but starts a completely new scene with new characters and new goals. Sometimes players off stage are looking for interesting body positions to assume. Sometimes they sense that the scene on stage is reaching an end or even failing. Whatever the reason, it is important to remember that all the improvisers are engaged even if they are not the ones in the scene. What collaboration. Many improvisers use freeze as a warm-up. However, I have also seen games of freeze go on for more than half an hour. The fun comes in seeing what ideas or offers the freezer makes, negotiating the chaos or change, and experimenting with different roles.

Sharing art work together, as play, stimulates and builds human relationships. As the participants in the study noted, some of their best friends are their fellow improvisers. Furthermore, through their play they felt they learned how to share, trust, and listen. Although many remember being taught these things in kindergarten, wouldn't it have been more fun to learn them through play? Those skills probably would have been more easily retained if learned rather than taught.

Collaboration spawns creativity. Yes, each person is creative, but mixing and blending individual creativity produces something more than the sum of the individual creativity. Apply this idea then to the classroom. I am not suggesting that teachers play freeze in class, well maybe I am, but more realistically I am suggesting collaboration and active listening. Just as improvisers should not become audience, neither should students. Instead, teachers should find ways to making the learning collaborative. I have been teaching for a long while now. I am the first to admit that I still have lots to learn. I can still be the teacher and not know everything or prove that I know everything by lecturing to my class. Teachers who set up a learning environment and foster a spirit of play within this environment have a greater potential for collaborative learning for everyone.

MAKING MISTAKES

The biggest error educators (and thus our current society) make is instilling a sense of shame associated with failure and mistakes. I have read the comparative analogy of the grain of sand in the oyster and the resultant pearl often given by champions of mistakes. Lovely as that idea is, that to obtain the pearl infers that it takes a long time to get to the reward. With improv, the failures are often quick. The improviser assesses the mistake and moves on. Rarely, in my experience, have I seen an improviser fall apart over a failed scene. My guess is that when coupled with a spirit of play the wins and losses are all part of the game and all worthy of enjoyment.

The difference lies in the lack of competitive play. Instead of worrying about wins and losses or outshining another actor, remember that one of the guidelines of improv is to make to other actor look good. Although the participants often described themselves as a team, they meant it as a collaborative team not a competitive one. This takes a great amount of trust and support, but the reward is a sense of empowerment rather than one of embarrassment. Improvisers always take care of each other, even if they are not in the scene. An example of this is the use of the *backline* improvisers. As in the example of the game of freeze, since the backline actors are engaged and not watching as audience, the backline has the potential to help scenes they perceive are in the process of failing. Often backline actors will insert themselves into the scene physically, adding a character or a motivation that moves a scene from potential failure. Other times, backline actors can insert their ideas by *side coaching* or providing information but not inserting themselves physically. An example of this is when a backline actor yells, "Cut to." In a scene, the characters might refer to an incident that happened outside the current scene. A backline actor could yell, "Cut to (that incident)!" The actors on stage (and any additional backline actors needed) switch immediately to the previously mentioned incident. The use of "cut to" side coaching helps move a failing scene. However, scenes can still fail on the actor level, the character level, and the group level. And it's okay.

I think of famous mistakes that many of us heard of as children (e.g., Fleming and the discovery of penicillin or Edison and the light bulb). I have seen improvisers use mistakes and failures to their advantage. Good improvisers learn how to take their mistakes and turn them into inspiration. Avoiding mistakes, playing it safe, does not make for interesting scenes. I am not saying to purposely aim for failure, but rather to take the moments that do not work out as intended and build out of them. Perhaps, I am advocating for the pearl analogy, here, but only as a beautiful product of failure not as an irritant that takes a long time to evolve. For improvisers, a better word for this evolutionary process of failure and polish is, simply, practice.

PRACTICING

Another adage I have trouble with is "Practice makes perfect". This might seem odd in that I just finished talking about the process of failure and the need to continually fail and make mistakes to move forward. The objection I have with the adage is that in striving for perfection, the practice can become dogmatic drudgery. Instead, the spirit of play needs to remain firmly in place throughout the practice and training process or the intrinsic rewards will not occur. Improvisers who focus on perfection while they practice cannot get out of their heads, and creativity ceases. The play element of chance is too pervasive in improvisation for there to be rigid, repetitive scene work. This might work for other art forms, such as scripted acting or symphonic music. I often have friends and family members ask me how improv can be practiced. It seems counter intuitive to them. What I tell them is that it is not the product that is rehearsed, but the process. Improvisers practice their skills and abilities and apply them to the framework of the game with which they are presented. Again, in my opinion, improvisation is a really good life skill since none of us really knows what the product of our lives will be.

As I mentioned practice can take on a negative feeling. Anyone who has played a musical instrument or sport probably remembers the boredom of practice drills. While many see practice as the means to the end (a performance), I argue that they are part and parcel of the same thing. In practicing the skills, in anything, we gain the techniques and abilities that allow us to...stop thinking. Don't get me wrong; I am not advocating for people to turn off their brains and run free with wild abandon. I am saying that creativity and innovation sometimes need the higher executive functions the brain provides to get out of the way. Unlike brainstorming, which does have some similar aspects, practiced improvising consists of more than "just anything" and filters it within the framework of the scene or game. As several of the participants of the study noted, this borders on therapy. That is why is it so important to build trust and a safe practice space for improv. In this safe space, improvisers can experiment and flex their creative muscles, learn from mistakes, and keep their art fresh. Practice for improvisers should be playing with all the nonjudgmental elements that go with playing.

Good practice, where the improvisers feel challenged and creative, becomes addictive. Many of the participants in the study said as much. Again it is important to remember that this is a positive life-fulfilling and not a life-draining addiction. The intrinsic rewards that an improviser achieves through practice feed their desire to keep practicing.

The participants in this study believed theatrical improvisation could benefit a person of any age. Although the findings from this study indicated that age of the emerging adult (Arnett, 2000) factored into the perceived developmental gains, the findings related to the phenomenon may be transferrable to high school or older adult learners. Future researchers might replicate this study within different age level learning environments. Additional phenomenological inquiry with different age groups could add insights into lifelong learning and the value of such experiences.

Using the conceptual framework of this study as a springboard, future researchers could examine different activities that adhere to a specific concept (e.g., improvisation and flow). Phenomenological studies into other arts with improvisational experiences (i.e. instrumental jazz music, dance, or painting) at the college level would reveal more about the phenomenon of improvisation. Along a similar strategy, researchers with a focus on flow activities could investigate other flow extracurricular activities at college campuses to extend the findings from this study.

Finally, variations on the research design would add to the findings from this study or yield different findings. A quantitative survey of multiple college campuses could reveal more about theatrical improvisational opportunities for college students across the country to see if, and how, other institutions support the activity. A longitudinal study similar to Foubert and Urbanski's (2006) but specifically examining theatrical improvisers over the course of their college careers would reveal similar findings of psychosocial development. While great changes to the research design of this study would require greater leaps of faith in confirming my findings, even small changes such a different sample could strengthen the findings and, therefore, the implications of this study.

Adding to my idea that anyone can do improv, I believe anyone can find pleasure in doing so, thus justifying the activity. So often these days, the answer to the question of why people do things is met with an obligatory answer of necessity. With the focus of money gain that is so prevalent in today's culture, doing something because it's fun holds little water. I disagree with this idea. Instead of filling our young people's heads with goals of benchmarks to be met, I believe they should learn how to find how to motivate themselves, how to fail, how to be human, and how to cooperate with each other. While these sound like things one would learn at an early age, this tutelage tends to end after kindergarten. Again, how sad. And if we as citizens continue to place a schism between work and fun, we will have a society of unhappy, unhealthy adults. In the next chapter, I describe ways in which people can discover the power of improvisation for themselves and apply them to their lives.

Chapter Ten

Finding Improv in the Everyday

"Improv helps with acting and teaching and any field where you have to interact with another human being. There is no situation in which you wouldn't need to listen to or you wouldn't need to actually hear what another person was saying and pay attention to every little detail."
—Donnie (pseudonym, study participant)

In this chapter, I describe how improvisational strategies and principles can be inserted into different areas of our lives. I do so in hopes of providing answers to my call for instilling people's lives with more fun and more meaningful play. The ideas presented in this chapter come from the study and from my own experiences; they are meant to be illustrative not exhaustive or exclusive.

FOR EDUCATORS

I have made the connection between improv and play, but will continue to do so, not to belabor the point, but to continue to validate both as important to humanity. Throughout our educational journeys, most people can remember one educator (if they are lucky) that they felt really made a difference in their lives. I was lucky to have had two. The first one I mentioned in the preface of the book was my middle school drama teacher, Judy. The second was my high school calculus teacher. While it may be obvious how my drama teacher influenced me, it took reflection and discussion between my classmates and this math teacher (as adults) to help me to understand why he was such a great teacher (yes, we all still talk with each other 20 years later).

For the purpose of this book, I will call this teacher, simply, Dan. Dan taught calculus. As high school seniors in the 1980s, our focus was on the

Advanced Placement Exams. Dan knew this and daily would remind us of our goal to get top scores on that exam. However, while that was his message, and sounds a great deal as if he was teaching to the test, Dan did more than prepare us for a test. He prepared us for anything. Dan fostered innovation, creativity, and most of all community within his class. We worked for a common goal; we learned how to learn from each other; and we learned how to make mistakes. Dan may have appeared to outside observers as a "Sage on the Stage" imparting formulas and theorems to us (while pantomiming practicing his golf swing), but this was only part of the picture. The camaraderie we felt as a class has continued to serve us throughout our adult lives. Basically, Dan taught us to improvise and the "game" we were playing was calculus.

I realize this sounds odd. The class was calculus, and we did learn calculus. However, as in any improv game, Dan approached it with a spirit of fun. He set parameters (rules), yet we did whatever we wanted within the framework of those rules. One of my classmates was notorious for solving problems differently from everyone else. Dan never said, "No." He followed the rule of acceptance and, more importantly, helped the class support our out-of-the-box thinking classmate. I had an idiosyncratic behavior in that class that Dan still reminds me of regularly: I moved around his classroom, sitting in different seats each class throughout the school year. Dan never said anything to me about it (at the time, although he always had to hunt for me when taking attendance) and accepted it. Other teachers were not as supportive. I believe they felt threatened by my daily movement and thought it added to the classroom chaos. Dan trusted me to not disrupt the class, which I didn't, and passed that sense of trust to the rest of the class. Having been told I could not do that in other classes, I felt less a part of those classes and less motivated. Listening to and conferring with my former classmates, years later, we all determined that Dan could have taught us any subject; the key aspects of his teaching included his ability to engage us and excite us. Going to calculus was fun (really). Dan provided us with a learning environment that focused on the three principles of improvisation: trust, presence, and acceptance. Using these principles in the context of any subject matter could improve student engagement and overall learning.

Lobman and Lundquist (2007) argued experienced teachers differ from their novice counterparts in the degree to which they improvise in their classes. Perhaps, novice teachers fear the chaos that leaving a scripted curriculum might create. Perhaps, experienced teachers know their curriculum so well they can leave the script. Both of these thoughts may be true, but researchers have shown the positive influences teachers have on their students when they infuse their teaching with the spirit of play and improvisation. Educators who take the time to lift their eyes from their lesson plans begin to see their students. Using Howard Gardener's (1990) theory of multiple intelligences, the idea that one curriculum fits all is absurd. Only through a collaborative process can educators begin to understand how their students tick. Using improvisation, either through actual games (Appendix B) or just the basic tenets, educators can tap into their students' creativity and further discover what motivates them to learn more.

Another important aspect of improvisation that emerged from the study was the idea of practice. I stated it before, but it bears repeating. All of the participants from the study noted that whatever the overall benefits they witnessed from their experiences with improv, they all believed continual practice was essential. "A lot of people don't like getting up in front of other people, and I think that that shows that those muscles aren't very often flexed," said one participant. Just as a muscle needs to be worked, the improvisers from this study believed that their improvisational skills need continual attention and work. Educators who rely on the same method of instruction, the same curriculum, or the same answers set themselves up for boredom for not only themselves but for their students as well. Again, the theory of flow fits the idea of a need to continually challenge oneself (and others). By challenging others, I do not intend this in a confrontational manner. Remember another tenet of improvisation is to make your scene partner look good. For educators, listening to the students, championing their ideas (offers), and trusting them to add to the collect learning process are ways to challenge students and still make them look good. While the rules of improv can act as guidelines and inform educator choices, when first including improvisation games or strategies into the classroom, I recommend assuming the role of a coach. This level of collaboration is necessary, in the beginning, to build a space of trust.

Many of the games and strategies require a large amount of silliness; this is part of the fun. At first, the silliness and high potential for failure can act as deterrents to educators trying to achieve positive effects. As in the study, introducing improv to those who have not experienced or been trained in it before requires the hook of fun and inclusion. The spirit of play, particularly in the beginning, is imperative. This means that educators need to make sure everyone is aware of both the rules of improv and of the specific game. Furthermore, educators need to perform these games in a safe environment. For an environment to be safe, this means not only the physical area, but the emotional and social areas are also safe for the students. Students bruise easily–their bodies, their egos, and their emotions. I always begin introductory session, telling participants that they will make fools of themselves (as will I), that at some point one or all of us will fail, and that they should watch out for each other. After saying those things, I always ask them to keep what we say and do sacred to the confines of the room in which we are doing improv. By doing this, I believe this gives students the ability to feel safe and to try things they normally would not do. As noted by several of the participants of the study, improv walks a fine line between fun and therapy. It is the educator's responsibility to keep the games and the improvisational scenes on the "fun" end of the continuum and not towards the psychological end.

FOR THEATRE ARTISTS

Viola Spolin's (1987) seminal work, *Improvisation for the Theater*, focused on exercises for actors and directors to dig deeper into scripted characters, to free the inner artist, and to explore their own creativity. I do not understand why so many theatre artists I have met do not recognize the legitimacy of improvisation as an art form firmly planted in the field of theatre. I acknowledge that there are many ways to approach a play and that there are many ways to entertain an audience, not all good. However, the ability to improvise is an inherent part of being human. If theatre shows us the human condition, improvisation needs to be part of the conversation.

As an actor, I always relied on my improv training as a source of innovation and insight. A playwright can give an actor the words. A director can give an actor the flavor and color to go with the words. It is only the actor who can make each performance special and find the soul of the piece, night after night. Again, this ties to the theory of flow and the idea that skill and challenge need to be matched to attain optimal enjoyment. Actors practice and practice their lines and movements so that they become almost rote, but unless they are performing solo in a closed theatre, no performance can ever be exactly the same. Plays become a conversation between the actors, and the actors and the audience. While performances are fairly predictable, as in any conversation, changes to the dialogue can occur. Actors grow when they are faced with such challenges, otherwise boredom sets in (which an audience can feel). Actors need to adhere to the principles of improvisation whether they are improvising or performing a scripted piece. They have to be present as the actor and the character on the stage. I make the analogy of driving a car or any activity which may allow one's mind to wander. The actor has to be in the moment on the stage and not "adjusting the radio," or the illusion is lost. Actors need to accept offers made to them, by fellow actors, artists, and the audience. I once saw an actor stop a play to chastise an audience member who was talking during the performance. While I understood it, I never forgave her for breaking character and not working harder to try and draw in that audience member. Instead, that particular actor basically said, "No." For me it ruined the art of the moment and showed me the actor wanted to hear herself perform rather than share her art with the audience. That moment, when this actor stopped the play, also illustrated the principle of trust for me. Part of the principle of trust is making people, other than yourself, look good. As I have said, plays are conversations. An actor who does not trust their audience is not looking for a conversation; it is self-indulgent and not theatre, in my mind. Skilled improvisers who also perform scripted plays seem to be able to grasp the idea of theatre as conversation and art much better than actors who simply like to be seen. So, which actor is the better artist and rightly deserves a seat at the theatrical table? If you've been present and listening, you will know my answer. Improvisation will continue to be classified as merely a joke until theatre artists accept that improv is the soul of the theatre and not a mechanism to make the audience laugh. Laughter, tears, even cries of hatred will occur in a production if artists embody the principles of improvisation to their work. As the participant, Donnie, noted, improvisation is a selfless art form making it essential to theatrical experiences.

FOR ANYONE

Here is where I bring back Fox, the participant who met the sample criteria as stated but did not do improvisation as a college student. Much of what Fox said during the data collection sessions echoed the sentiments of his troupe mates; however, Fox found improv much later in his life. Many years ago, after reading a small ad for improv classes in a newspaper, Fox decided to enroll for a yearlong course. As mentioned in the methodology section of this book, this was in the Midwestern United Stated as what was then one of the incubating centers for improvisation. Fox had the good fortune to be able to travel for free from his home in the mid-Atlantic region to take these classes in the mid-West. Listening to Fox tell stories of those days would make any improviser jealous. Hearing how those times influenced Fox's life can inspire anyone to try to incorporate improvisation into one's life. After an 8-year hiatus from improv, Fox picked up *Guru* by Del Close. "God, I miss this. This was so much fun," Fox remarked to himself and promptly signed up for a local improv class. To date, Fox is part of several teams including The Society.

I took the opportunity to follow-up with Fox a year after the study ended. He continues to have amazing stories. I am struck by his overall good-natured quality, his willingness to share, and his slow smart sense of humor. When questioned, Fox did not recognize how all his experiences with improvisation had influenced his life, but to meet with him and talk with him I discerned that he embodied the principles of improv. Fox had applied all the rules and ideas of improv to his life. Fox lives his life in the present. My favorite tip Fox provided me with was "make friends with the janitor." Again, on the surface, it may not seem relevant to improv. Upon closer examination, I can see trust, presence, and acceptance. The idea harkens back to the selflessness for which improv stands. Furthermore, the concept of making friends with people that may otherwise not be in your normal circle of friends opens you up to more possibilities and makes your world bigger. These are things that will always be needed if humans are to continue to exist in this world. Not everyone will be a star and perform improv for a career; however, everyday everyone will improvise.

The next chapter is an informal study of applied improvisation professional. Six applied improvisers volunteered to talk with me about their work and improvisation. These people use the principles of improvisation to train, consult, and develop organizations and individuals.

Chapter Eleven

Applied Improvisation

"Improvisation is being applied in astonishing ways all over the world."
—Rebecca (Applied Improvisation Professional)

INTRODUCTION TO APPLIED IMPROVISATION

In the last chapter, I gave examples of where and how people can infuse improvisation and a spirit of play into different areas of life. Although the study focused on an academic environment with insights into students' perceptions on how improvisation influenced their education, the participants described how the principles and process of improvisation could influence other areas of their lives. While I had made these connections for myself and reviewed literature on organizational improvisation, I had not given much thought to applying the principles of improvisation to the larger community. To my surprise, there are a growing number of professionals who have made applied improvisation their life's work. According to one interviewee, the number of applied improvisation practitioners listed on the Applied Improv Network has grown from 200 to 5000 over the period of 12 years. For this chapter, I interviewed six professionals who identify themselves as working in this field, some of whom have been applying improvisation to promote development and self-awareness for over 25 years. I present their information and insights as an informal study.

Improvisation as form or branch of the theatre has been around for several decades. Improv has evolved and changed through practices and performances. As mentioned earlier in the book, within the field of theatre, improvisation has been used as a tool and generally overlooked as an art form unto itself. Over the past decade, comedic improvisation, as seen at local improv theatre or on television, has become more mainstream. However, an undercurrent of improv has persisted in areas outside of the theatre. When organizations and businesses needed staff development or team building, improvisers saw that they had the training and capacity to perform that training. As in the study, in the theme of Applications and Rewards, those who practice and train in improvisation can potentially make gains to their social and personal skills. Before describing applied improv in this way, I have presented how to apply improv to education, to theatre, to personal rewards—this is applied improv. However, when most people speak of applied improv, they intend it for the corporate and business world. To make the connection of my study to the larger community, I interviewed several people who identify themselves as applied improvisational professionals to gain insights into the applications of improvisation. In this chapter, I present the information from the interviews as an informal case study. Of interest to me were how these professionals echoed similar sentiments as the participants from the formal study. In this chapter, I provide their perceptions on their work, the principles of improvisation, and the future of applied improvisation.

INTRODUCTION TO THE PROFESSIONALS

I interviewed six applied improvisation professionals from across the United States. Some I found through the Applied Improvisation Network, but most were referrals from other professionals. All but one operated their own businesses training and facilitating using improvisation; the one professional works with an improvisation theatre as its improvisation training manager. Several of the others also work with or have worked with an improvisational theatre. All of their names and contact information can be found in the resources section of this book. These professionals come from different backgrounds. Some are trained actors, educators, social scientists, and even a self-proclaimed failed stand-up comic. They have varying degrees of education. They have varying views on what style of improv they prefer. They have differing ideas of where their profession should go (mostly). What do they have in common is their belief in the transformative powers of the process of improv, their love of their work, their commitment to fun and creativity, and their generous empowering of others. For the purposes of this book, I will refer to them by their first names. A list of their full names, companies, and titles can be found in the resources sections of this book. Already, it should be clear that they have applied the principles of improv to themselves and embody these principles.

PRINCIPLES OF IMPROV AND THE APPLICATIONS

In the formal study, while the participants described skills, abilities, and qualities they developed through improv, the students were reluctant to describe the rules or principles they identified as necessary to improvisation. I did not experience this reluctance when interviewing the applied improv professionals. Most of them had several principles and described using them in different ways as the situation demanded. Of interest, although the professionals describe the principles slightly differently, the common ideas that I have presented throughout this book (i.e., acceptance, trust, and presence) match those principles which the interviewees provided.

Acceptance

To the person, the applied improvisers gave the rule of *yes, and* as a core principle of their work. In the following statement, Chris described his perception of what *yes, and* means and does not mean.

> Suffice it to say this principle is a frequently used. In terms of all the ways I apply it, I could write my own book chapter on this concept alone. It is the underpinning for several other principles which build on this foundation. YES—acceptance, acknowledgement, admiration, appreciation, respect—not necessarily "agreement," which is what onstage improv might require
> AND - build on, add to, expand, advance, progress, imagine, contribute, embellish, pivot, adapt, hold space for conflicting points of view, begin collaboration. Together, they increase participation, flow, openness, tolerance and respect for different points of view, generate with synergy, construct positively, provide a framework for constructive communication, and conversation.

All of the interviewees stressed the importance of the combination of the two words and that the principle does not blanketly represent agreement. Michelle equated *yes, and* as being generative and moving away from what she determined as a "binary, right/wrong, good/bad" way of thinking into possibilities. To take the *yes, and* principle only as agreement strips it of its transformative potential. Sue, the most senior of the professionals I interviewed, noted from her experiences that sometimes understanding the principles of improvisation transcended knowing how to improvise and knowing the language that accompanies improv. In the following statement, Sue described how the use the language of improvisation without a full comprehension its role in the process impacted negatively on the experience.

> The language you use comes from your experience and your interpretation. I think you could go wrong (as a facilitator or leader) if you don't clarify to a client that the *yes* doesn't mean agreement. If you leave a client thinking *yes, and* means agreement, rather than realize *yes, and* is jargon that means accep-

tance, appreciation, encouragement, and respect…if you don't clarify that, then it can cause problems. It certainly causes resistance, and you won't get past it.

The other interviewees had similar ideas about how they applied the principle of *yes, and*. For John, the principle of yes, and was about appreciating and honoring the contribution, about an invitation to move forward, and about "talking with one another instead of at one another." Throughout the interviews of the six professionals, I noted that while they talked about their work with others as they applied their principles of improvisation, they also spoke of how the principles affected them personally. Lisa described herself as a person who naturally blocks or negates. "I've gotten better over the years at seeing how I can say, 'yes' to things because of this work," stated Lisa. When asked about how the interviewees came into the profession, many of them described instances when a friend or a former student referred them to teach or facilitate for a corporate or nontheatre organization. Rather than negating, they accepted and then worked on determining how best to serve their new audience. By following the principle of *yes, and* in their own lives, they transformed from teachers, performers, and other professionals to applied improv practitioners who opened up new opportunities for themselves. *Yes, and* falls firmly into the category of acceptance. I have split the other principles these professional described into the categories of trust and presence. Through hearing their description of what they believed were the core principles, I sensed a feeling of consensus between the interviewees that the lines between the principles blur and cannot stand alone.

Trust

Under my categorization of the principles of improv, I identified several rules of improv as described by the interviewees that fall in the category of trust. The first involves failing. Michelle described her relationship to failure in the following statement:

> It is absolutely transformative for individuals. In my case, while I had loved being creative privately or with friends, I was extremely shy with doing anything in public. Improv helped me break out of my shyness shell, be more co-creative, and be publicly creative. By messing up consistently in front of people, performing improv, and it being part of the fun, you just develop a new relationship to publicly making mistakes. It doesn't have a hold on you. I developed a new relationship to my fear of failure. I noticed that about all improvisers—the fear failure doesn't have big heavy baggage like it does "pre-improv" or for a lot of people I work with. I went from deeply fearing failure to seeing it as an invitation to create, an iteration in the creative process – what I used to see as "failure" became an iteration, and an invitation to create something new.

The interviewees noted that in most situations where they work, reprogramming people to embrace failure becomes one of their top priorities. Again, this ties to the theory of the balance of play elements. Our society, in the United States, is heavily situated in competitive play. Losing, making mistakes, and failing bring a sense of shame. Lisa noted this as well in this statement:

> I feel, in America, we're really driven to succeed and driven to work really, really hard. And there's not a lot of room for error. There's not a lot of room for mistakes. Sometimes what can happen is people stop being bold. Then, they become complacent. They become resentful, and ingenuity and innovation halt because people are afraid that their ideas are not going to be accepted. When we start to fail good naturally or to take risks and be bold, we can go back to being innovators. We can ideate in ways that are much more profound because we know that our ideas are going to be heard and, if not fully embraced, the catalysts for the next idea.

This idea of failing good naturally only works in conjunction with the principle of *yes, and*. Ideas, good, bad, or neutral need to have a fighting chance before getting shot down. They are offers and gifts in a scene and in life. Having the support of the group to recognize the offers as gifts helps people move forward and be creative. Most of the professionals I interviewed noted that helping their clients view failure in a positive way has led to radical changes in company cultures.

This idea of failing good naturedly ties into the next idea given to me by the interviewees. The participants in the study also identified this principle as influential to their development—make your scene partner look good. The applied improvisation professions took this principle and expanded it in their practices. Yes, the applied to their work in the groups, and they have their clients try to apply it to their work and their lives outside of work. Essentially, these professionals use this principle as a mission statement of their work—make their clients look better. Some of them included the idea of serving the scene or serving the whole, but most of them identified all the different aspects of the principle as moving towards a more selfless frame of mind and into one that focuses on improving the collective good. Michelle noted this:

> It's like situational leadership. Sometimes, it means you run in and support something that was just said. Sometimes, it means you run in and break a pattern or enhance something that is already there. Sometimes you don't interfere. If you're serving the scene, you're more likely to instinctively know what to do than if you are thinking, "How am I going to go in there and make the audience laugh?" Improv is a team sport. You do what's best for the team. The irony is when you commit to serving the scene over a solo agenda, what emerges is better, funnier, more coherent, and more creative than any one

person trying to make themselves look good. This principle is also true in work teams.

All of these principles work in conjunction with one another. Trusting your scene mates involves trusting yourself as well as supporting others so they can feel safe. The professionals I interviewed identified other principles, which I placed in third category of presence. Already, it should be evident that presence requires acceptance and trust to achieve.

Presence

For most of the interviewees, the principle of presence came in different forms. For Chris, presence appeared in his principles of *silencing your inner judge, noticing more, listening, responding, and adapting.* Sue described that being fully present was the undercurrent attitude that carried all of her work. John noted that being present and focusing on what is said is needed in all areas of society. "There's a real need for some core competencies in our society," stated John, "for hearing one another, for listening to one another fully, and for working constructively together." Michelle had this to say about applied improvisation and presence:

> Improv increases your capacity for presence and presenting. Being here—now. When you are present, you have access to infinitely more creativity then when you're not present. You're more alert and aware of what's happening around you. You can respond from a more conscious place instead of from autopilot. That impacts the choices and decisions you'll make.

If you are not fully present or in the moment, how can you serve the scene? I mention elsewhere in the book about acting from the backline. It's the job, the point of concentration, of an improviser to help their scene mates. Listening and watching, what goes on in the scene forces players into the now and makes them more mindful. Improv is selfless and, yet, self-aware—serving the group while affecting and transforming the self.

THEMES

Although the principles of the professionals had commonality, as with their backgrounds, the styles and forms of improv the professionals I interviewed varied greatly. Several noted a firm grounding in Boal's and Johnstone's work. Others followed, more, the style of the comedic improvisation as developed by Close. John described himself as a "journeyman," taking different bits and pieces of the craft from the different places in which he had studied. Of note, most of the professionals began as performers and some of them still perform with improv groups regularly. However, they were unified on what they were doing in their profession was not teaching improvisation with the intent of fostering performers. Instead, they teach the principles of improv and their applications. In line with the idea of *serving the whole*, many of the professionals described creating workshops and session purely based on the needs of the client. Furthermore, many said they do not rigidly plan sessions or workshops; they come with basic ideas but a wealth of games and exercises they use as they see fit the needs of the group at that moment (again, practicing the same principles that they teach). I am reminded of the statement I made earlier in the book countering the adage of "those who can't do teach." I wish to restate my opinion for emphasis using these six individuals as evidence for my claim: Being a teacher or leader does not mean a person cannot perform the task or skill that is taught. In fact, artists that teach their craft give the gift of their experiences to their students beyond what can be learned from printed material or theoretical study.

Flow

While flow is not a style of improv, as shown by the data in this study, improvisation can be highly conducive to flow. The interviewees for this chapter identified several skills they targeted with their use of the core principles. Understanding that when people's skills meet the challenge at hand the result is an optimal state of being, applied improv practitioners could augment the potential enjoyment of their clients by balancing those dynamics. Rebecca said this about making the connection between skill and challenge:

> The principles lead to people paying attention to each other and connecting. That's what teams are made of. Team building is just sort of inherent, and creativity is just inherent because you're being spontaneous and playful— ideas flow like water.

The analogy between being in the moment and flowing like water came up a lot in both the interviews with the study participants and the interviews with the applied improv professionals. As with the naming of the core principles, although diverse, all of the descriptions had a similar thread—fun and enjoyment. Csikszentmihalyi (1991) noted that not everyone achieves flow in all situations. However, the potential for flow like experiences are great in improv, and the experiences of flow (whether recognized or not) result in enjoyment. John described his journey of becoming an applied improviser as beginning with falling in love with improv in this statement:

> I had done some improv in college. Several years later, as a faculty member, I decided to pick it back up. For me, it was just going to be a fun hobby, something that I would enjoy. And then I went down the rabbit hole of improv and fell dearly and completely in love with it.

This idea of embracing the fun of improv and developing a relationship with the challenges and skills that accompany improvisation make people want to do more improv. John's analogy of going "down the rabbit hole of improv" resonated with me. After hearing about the work that these professionals do with improvisation, I too began to believe it may be a solution to world peace. If not world peace, at least if more people adhered to the principles of improvisation and challenged themselves more to be creative and spontaneous, we might all have a little more fun.

Play and Not Play

I clearly heard from the six people I interviewed that they enjoyed their work. Many felt that helping others to understand improvisation and apply it to other areas of their lives fed their souls. It has been the life work of some of the interviewees even when the term, applied improvisation, did not really exist. These people have found the spirit of play with which they have infused their lives, their work, and by extension, the lives and work of others. "It's so heartwarming to me," said Sue, "to know that this work has that kind of an impact on people and that it lasts." As applied improv professionals, the interviewees described playing with the principles and structure of improvisation to meet the needs of their clients. In the following statement by Michelle, one can see her relationship to a spirit of play and the principle of *yes, and*:

> *Yes* builds the bridge, but the *and* keeps it generative. The *yes* is the connection. The *and* is the obligation to play…As applied improvisers, we're being invited to play with the structure of how a group or organization works…I like the play format (of improv) because it allows you a larger space to engage in the unknown.

By playing through the unknown in a collaborative manner, the interviewees believed that applied improvisation has the potential for positive social change.

VIEWS ON THE FUTURE OF APPLIED IMPROVISATION

I noted that, while the profession of an applied improvisation facilitator or leader is relatively new to me, people have made the connection of the principles of improvisation and applied them outside of the theater for as long as improv has been around. So I asked the six professionals what they hoped for the future of their profession. All of them passionately believed in the transformative power of improvisation to affect positive social change. Chris said, "My intuition tells me, it (applied improvisation) will only increase in mainstream acceptance, as best practice and more awareness grow around this emerging field." As to whether there should be a certification or standardization of the profession, all of them had mixed feelings.

Rebecca said, "Every time the conversation of certification comes up (at professional conferences), it gets really muddy, really fast." Reviewing the backgrounds of how these professionals became applied improvisers and listening to them describe their work helps to understand the group's mixed views.

A Calling

Due to the relative newness of the profession, only a few institutions of higher education offer degrees in applied theatre. Even fewer offer classes in applied improvisation. For the interviewees, I had the sense that they felt "called" to the profession. However, I believe the groundwork of service supported their leap into the perceived chaos of improvisation. Several of the interviewers were educators, in some fashion, prior to their journey into the profession. Some stated they started out looking for a way to help others find creativity and joy in their lives and wanted to shared their craft. Each story I heard from these six people had an element of passion for the art and for their fellow human. It sounds pretty noble and pretty silly, especially when you juxtapose what they hope to achieve with what many believe are frivolous parlor games. The paradox I noted in Chapter 5 between play and any potential benefits should be seen as the "red thread" throughout the book. The idea that someone can be called to serve their fellow human through applications of improvisation, might seem ridiculous but should be given the same care and consideration as any profession. Michelle said this about being called to a profession:

> My deeper philosophical viewpoint is that there comes a time when you do what is yours to do—you serve in the way that is unique and alive for you. Following your calling is like following a thread on in an improv scene: You respond, listen, answer, and do what's yours to do.

A Profession

For these six people, being an applied improvisational professional has been as unpredictable as improvisation itself. Only in the past few years, has improv become as mainstream in our culture. When working with clients outside the field of theatre or improvisation, Sue and Rebecca both noted the need to avoid using theatre terms or even the word, *improv*, because the clients panic or take the workshops less seriously. Sue noted these reactions happened more in the earlier days of her practice in the 1980s but still happen today in some instances. Others have been able to capitalize on the rising tide of acceptance for improvisation. Listening to the clients and determining how to best serve them and meet their needs, helps perpetuate facilitation of applied improv workshops. Creating a network of likeminded professionals was the first step in coalescing the field and proving its practitioners with credibility and validation. However, as the field continues to gain recognition, its practitioners face the growing question of whether or not to standardize, certify, or brand their practice.

Standardization/Certification

One of the aspects of improvisation that the college students from the study noted is the inclusive nature of the craft. The participants from the study approached improv with a sense of fun and openness; for The Society, no audition process was needed. While this may be true for people who do improv, standardization and certification become a legitimate question for people who apply improvisation as their career. The issue of standardization becomes a tricky one. As Lisa noted:

> I think if there were some level of standards, it could lend more credibility to what we do…It could open doors; it could also close doors. One of the things I loved (coming into this career) is having a master's degree in teaching, having experience in the world, having a passion for improv, and having curiosity, which allowed me to create the business I have today. No one stopped me, and I would hate to stop anyone else.

A few of the interviewees confessed that they thought they were the first ones to think of applying improv principles. These people developed their own programs independently of the network. While the different styles and formats of improvisation make it seem as though standardization might be impossible, the core principles remain the same. "There is an enormous amount of things that fall under the label of applied improv," said John. "Practitioners, even though they share the same label, have radically different expertise and knowledge that they are bringing to the field." John's statement identifies the diversity of the practitioners and the potential downside of a lack of standards.

"My personal viewpoint of improvisation finds beauty in that there is no standardization," said Chris. "Part of the gift we offer is how to find newness, openness, creativity, flexibility, and comfort with ambiguity. Standardization, somehow, seems to lessen the potential upside of improvisation." Chris identified the inherent aspect of improv as fluid and the benefits of that fluidity. I combine these two thoughts with the principle of *yes, and,* over which I doubt any of the interviewees would argue too strongly. *Yes,* the openness, fluidity, and spontaneity of improvisation can pervade with the work done with applied improvisation, *and* a degree of standardization can be established for its practitioners. Although my disbelief in the adage of those who cannot do teach might seem counterintuitive, I also feel that not everyone who can do can teach. While I believe anyone can improvise, leading others and helping them to comprehend the potential transformative powers of improvisation take practice and skill. For Sue, making sure that new applied improvisers have facilitation training has been part of her objective with the Applied Improvisation Network.

"My focus has been to take the new people (to the field) who have this enthusiasm and this love of the process," said Sue, "and show them how to be effective facilitators. If we can just objectify the process, then people can grow their skills." Several of the professionals I interviewed suggested the idea of guidelines for the practice rather than certification. Furthermore, most of the interviewees noted that adherence to the core principles of improvisation and their application to the profession itself could help unify the field. As a word of caution for the executive or human resource person who may have picked up this book in the hope that they could gain more information on applied improv and how it could help their organization, not everyone who has taken improvisation classes can teach others.

"Real harm can be done," stated John, "if it (applied improvisation) is handled badly." Do your homework when hiring any professional. Just because people claim to be something, does not make it so. That being said, the potential good that can come from applied improvisation can be great. The practitioners with whom I interviewed all felt strongly about the potential of applied improvisation for positive social change. I present those thoughts, along with the impacts of the formal study in the final chapter of this book. In the next chapter, I provide an overview of games and strategies I have used and describe how I use them.

Chapter Twelve

Improv Games and Exercises Overview

"We have games that will intentionally put you out of your comfort zone, which is good because it helps you grow."
—Lester (pseudonym, study participant)

I include this chapter to give readers an idea of how I have used these games and strategies in my classroom, my improv workshops, and my organizational development seminars. I offer them as suggestions. My sample of games (Appendix B) is not exhaustive or even comprehensive, merely illustrative. The games and strategies have come to me from students, books, the internet, and other places. I wish I could give credit to the originators; I will attribute games when I know their origin. However, since the games come from all over the world and from different theaters and troupes, some may not be attributed. Improvisers pass games along and are generous with their sharing. Improvisation is fluid and dynamic. Furthermore, I may take a game and adapt it to suit the group or the situation. Some games are easy and give quickly realizable results. Others are more challenging. The principle of flow applies to improv: skill level needs to meet challenge, if optimum enjoyment is to occur. Trying hard games first will bring frustration and anxiety. The examples given in the appendix are easy to do at any level. Easy games played by those with more experience could produce boredom and should be adapted appropriately. When I lead a workshop or a class, I always try to gauge my class to the participants' needs and their experience levels. I do so with sociometric exercises.

SOCIOMETRICS

Developed by Moreno for his work in sociodrama in the 1930s (Blatner, 2009; Dayton, 2005), sociometric exercises engage players by asking them to move their bodies in the space in response to questions posed to them by the leader. Boal (2002) and Fox (1994) used elements of sociometrics as part of their style of improv. The use of sociometric exercises accomplishes several things. First, as mentioned above, they provide the leader with the opportunity to gain more information about the group and its individuals. Second, sociometric exercises begin the process of inclusion by giving the players a task that they can focus on and that does not make them stand out from the group. Many people express a fear of improv as needing to perform and to be funny. Sociometric exercises break the ice between the players and begin the process of getting them in the moment. Third, through several sociometric exercises, a group (established or a group of strangers) starts to create its own entity or social atom (Moreno, 2008). There have been instances when I have only used sociometric exercises for a session or workshop. In the study, the participants described the theme of The Hook, the part that drew of improv which drew them in and engaged them. Sociometric exercises can do just that as can warm-up exercises.

WARM-UP EXERCISES

Athletes stretch and warm-up before playing a game or exercising. Singers warm-up their voices before singing. These are just a few examples I give when I am asked by players why they need to do warm-ups (particularly after I have done sociometric exercises with them). The sociometric exercises help me determine what the group needs (i.e., do they lack energy, are they not focusing, are they intimidated by the group, or do they need more introduction to each other). Warm-ups can be used to stimulate the body, the mind or to relax either. Warm-ups can also simply be fun. Games that I use for warm-ups are generally are non-completive in nature. The non-competitive nature of improvisation and games with no "winner" help balance out the elements of play as noted by Caillois (1958). Today's culture is highly competitive; activities that promote collaboration and cooperation help people counter this effect while also teaching social competency. Again, particularly in warm-up activities, the focus needs to be on having fun.

PRESENCE EXERCISES

Sociometric and warm-up exercises begin the process that includes nurturing the other skills. Furthermore, the games often work on more than one skill, I use the terms, *games* and *exercises*, almost interchangeably but acknowledge the differences between the two. Games usually have rules and structure with the goal of a scene in mind. Exercises are activities that focus on specific principles or rules on which to work. However, this gets muddy too, as games can also focus on one or more principle as the participants from the study noted in the theme of The Craft. Working with players on presence, the goal of the activities is to get the players to shutout the outside worries and cares they may have brought in with them. Additionally, presence exercises can help develop skills in two different ways. Following Spolin's (1987) idea of point of concentration (POC), players need to have a job or a POC within an improv scene. Doing so draws the players into the moment of the scene and out of their heads. Nachmanovitch (2010) described the internal self-judging humans do as "the judging spectre" (p. 133). I have also heard this called "police in your head." Without training or even practice, humans have a tendency to filter or pre-evaluate how they are going to move and speak. Outside of improvisation, this may be a good thing. However, within improvisation, the cop in your head can kill any creative activity for which improv stands. In my experiences teaching, I find giving students a POC within a scene tends to keep the inner judge occupied so the unfiltered creative stuff can come out.

Although giving players a task in a game or a scene can help bring them more into the moment and make them less self-conscious, players need to do more than focus on one thing. Remembering the tasks and the rules, while still moving a scene forward, takes practice. I often try to have students and newcomers to improv pair with more experienced players. In this way, the newer players can rely on the more experienced player to move the scene while learning how to focus on their tasks and rules. Good improvisers make this look easy in a way I feel good swimmers make swimming look easy. Like improv, swimming should be something anyone could do but learning it, never having been in the water before, can feel a bit like one is drowning. It is good to have someone with you when you learn. Learning presence can be as simple as learning to rely on your scene partner. As Donnie remarked in the focus group, being in an improv scene can be like being in a bad combat situation (except for the potential loss of life). Those players in a scene may recognize a terrible situation or a scene going bad; however, they trust each other so much they believe they will not only get through the scene but may even be better for it. Although trust can be fostered and taught, as I suggest by presenting trust exercises, trust within the members of an improv group really needs to be cultivated and, ultimately, earned through shared experiences.

TRUST EXERCISES

The ability to trust others as well as one's self, does not come easily to adults. Perhaps, in a manner similar to our capacity to play, adults become less open, more guarded, and predisposed to judging as they get older. People can lessen their reactions, such as prejudging, by focusing on being in the moment. The more people react without running everything through a filter the more creative they can become. However, this also means people need to feel secure. The data from the study in which the participants described trusting their troupe mates spoke to their sense of security. The Society members felt secure because of the support of their troupe mates. Other data spoke to their sense of self-trust and confidence. Neither of these abilities (trusting others or one's self) can be developed in a 30-minute workshop. What can be taught is the reminder of how we as children trusted ourselves and others when we played. As I have mentioned before, I open any session, workshop, or class explaining that what happens in the class stays in the class, that one or all of the group will make a complete fool of themselves at some point, and that we will all survive it together. As a gauge, I use sociometric exercises, such as:

> Place yourself in the room. On this side (indicating one side) of the room if you feel very comfortable doing group exercises with the others in this group, and on this side of the room (pointing to the opposite side) if you are very uncomfortable. Think of the room as a line measuring your degree of comfort with very comfortable on this side (indicate the first side), very uncomfortable on this side (indicate the second side), or some place in between. There is no right or wrong answer. Judge for yourself. Move.

By doing this exercise, I can see how much of the session I need to spend on trust work. Building trust within a group is more easily accomplished using the trust exercises I provide in Appendix B than building participants' confidence. Confidence comes from practice and from repeatedly putting oneself out there. Acceptance from other players results when one has put oneself "out there" and represents one of the most important and most powerful aspects of improvisation for creativity, personal growth, and confidence building.

ACCEPTANCE EXERCISES

I have spoken about the power of acceptance, about the rule of *yes, and,* and about how this concept is one I consider a key tenet of improvisation. Saying, *no,* is easy. For most two-year-old children, *no,* comes out of their mouths more than anything else. Perhaps, that is because that is what they hear most often. In the world of improvisation, *no* stops everything. Using exercises to reinforce *yes, and*, have received a lot of negative reactions. A few years ago, a family member of mine had just finished a staff development workshop (applied improv) at his work. He related how much fun he and his colleagues had had mocking the *yes, and* exercises. In fact, he said it became a bit of a running joke within the office after the workshop when a member of the group wanted to have an inside laugh. I suppose in some ways the exercise did help build community in this instance (having a shared laugh); however, I have not shaken the feeling that once again improvisation was not regarded as a serious craft with real benefits. When an instructor uses acceptance exercises or teaches the principle in any other way when training others in improvisation, I feel it is important to accept that resistance will always be there. That it is easier to negate often because it brings a laugh, but true growth comes from accepting offers made by others. In addition, building on those offers makes them even better.

LEADER GUIDES

Everyone that leads improvisation has their own style. Here, I merely offer suggestions that have worked for me. I subscribe to side coaching as described by Viola Spolin (1987). By asking to players to listen to my words while playing a game or doing an exercise without turning their attention to me, I help players stay on the focus of the scene and help progress the scene. In many ways, side coaching follows the principle identified by the participants in the study: always make your partner look good. Through side coaching, leaders can help both the scene and the players. Additionally, as any good coach would do, a side coach helps the players realize their own potential and nurture innate abilities. I often tell the players to let me be the cop in their heads telling then when they are off task or when to wrap up a scene. When the instructor/leader assumes the role of *cop in the head*, players become more open to innovation. Working with an established group of improvisers, the need to side coach lessens or is assumed by the group. I mentioned side coaching for those doing applied improvisation.

My other suggestions for leaders are simpler to do. Make a safe environment for the group. Creativity and risk go hand in hand, but players still need to feel safe. Have fun. If you as a leader are not enjoying yourself, how can the rest of the group? Finally, believe in the process and the power of play. As Huizinga (1950) noted, humans are misnomered; we really should have been called *homo ludens* (man the player). In the final chapter of this book, I present the impacts and implications of the study and, as I see it, the inclusion of improvisation and fun into people's lives.

Chapter Thirteen

Serious Fun for Life

"Improv teaches folks to play well with one another under very frightening situations. I can't think of a better way to move forward as a society. When we play together as a society, it is increasingly frightening and has increasingly high stakes."
—John (Applied Improvisation Professional)

IMPLICATIONS OF THE STUDY: SO WHAT?

Throughout this book I have maintained that, while everybody improvises, by honing and practicing those skills anyone can experience joy and a sense of fulfillment. I think of it as play that is accessible to a person no matter their age. In general, humans are social creatures. Making connections with another human being enriches our lives. The study in this book focused on improvisation and education. Today's state of education makes me sad. I remember running to school, excited to learn. I also remember the sense of joy slowly leeching out of me as I got older. In my opinion, the point of education became one of a standardized product and not of the process of creating effective adults.

With this book and the study, I have provided scientific evidence that play matters, that improv means more to the actors than being silly, that joy can be found in losing oneself in the moment, and that there is still hope for the future of society that recognizes these things. Educational buzzwords come and go. Right now, attention is given to the term, *grit*. Duckworth, Peterson, Matthews, & Kelly (2007) described grit as long-term persistence and tenacity, which when examined in students could predict future success. I am not a grit scholar but am curious as to how humans learn grit. Future research could be done to determine if grit levels increased with improv training.

The study began with this question: How have experiences with improv training, practice, and performance helped college students make meaning of their ongoing development? For answers, I looked at a community college improv group that practiced and performed improv as an extracurricular activity. Because of the research findings, several areas appear where positive social change could happen. This study impacted individuals and groups within the context of this study. The participants through the descriptions of their experiences expressed feelings of change. The improvisational group, The Society, could change its role and structure at the college. The student affairs department and other college faculty and staff could witness positive social change in the form of increased student engagement. With this study, I also offer implications to the methodology and theory for the purposes of eliciting positive social change. Finally, in this section, based on my research, I make recommendations for changes to practices of the college with regard to student activities and potentially adult education in the hopes greater student engagement, motivation, and development within the context of the study.

IMPACTS

With this interpretive phenomenological study, I committed to investigating the essence (van Manen, 2014) and temporal manifestations (Vagle, 2014) theatrical improvisational experiences held for seven community college students and alumni as they reflected on their ongoing development. As a result, my research impacted the participants and the improvisation group with potential impact to the college and the larger community. Implications of the improvisers' choice to train, practice, and perform their craft as an extracurricular activity at a community college support such opportunities for student engagement and satisfaction.

Impact for the Participants

All of the participants expressed an eagerness to volunteer for this study and share their experiences with me. In Chapter 8, findings from the study described increased self-awareness of the participants concerning themselves, their craft, and their experiences with The Society. Through the participants' reflections, all of them described an increased appreciation for their troupe mates, and the role their experiences have had on their lives both in and out of college. The implications of positive social change for the participants lie in this increased self-awareness as well as their applications of their perceptions to other areas of their lives.

Impact for The Society

As the participants reflected on the aspects of The Society that attracted them to the group and on their perceptions of wanting to perform their craft, many of the participants reported increased insights into how The Society or if The Society should change its organizational structure. As an extracurricular activity, participants saw the group as an open, noncompetitive opportunity outside of their academic curriculum. However, through their reflections on their experiences, many of the participants expressed the desire to perform while at the same time acknowledging performance requires a certain level of training that not everyone in the group possessed. In addition to the performance aspect of The Society, a few participants described a lack of satisfaction with the requirements the student affairs department applied to all extracurricular activities. Positive social change for The Society would include a reorganization of the group to fit the needs of all group members for increased opportunities, increased membership, and increased energy for outreach.

Impact for the Research Site

The descriptions of the experiences speak to the awareness of the student affairs department and the college of what The Society provided and continues to provide students and community members. As previously mentioned, while all the participants expressed a sense of gratitude to the college for providing those experiences, a few participants perceived a lack of understanding by the college community of what The Society did, and how it functioned. The few participants with negative feelings argued that not all groups under the auspices of the department of student affairs should be treated the same way or conform to the same standards. At the college in this study, there existed no connection between The Society and the theatre department. Implications for positive social change at the college include increased awareness of both the positive and negative aspects of a theatrical improvisation group on the campus as a club or in connection to the academic program.

Impact for the Larger Community

Spolin (1987), Boal (2002), and Fox (1994) argued that theatrical improvisation helps to build community. In the context of this study as an extracurricular activity on a community college campus, any community member (not just students) could join The Society. Five of the participants in this study practiced, trained, and performed with The Society as alumni. The positive social change implications of open enrollment in student activities include an increased awareness of the college in general, which could, in turn, promote enrollment. Two of the alumni participants considered re-enrolling in classes to complete their associate's degrees. Performances by The Society provided another opportunity for community building on the campus. The participants described how they have acquired an audience following over the years. These performances bring community members to the campus who may not have come otherwise, thus increasing the scope of the college and providing the community with low cost entertainment. As a side note, the performing members of The Society donate their performance proceeds to charitable organizations.

IMPLICATIONS FOR METHODOLOGY
AND THEORETICAL CONCEPTS

The connections to the theoretical concepts and the findings that emerged from this research focus should, understandably, interest researchers and practitioners of theatrical improvisation, play, and flow. Regardless of their perceptions of competency in the craft, the choice faithfully to practice and train Friday evenings speaks to the intrinsic rewards the participants described with their experiential accounts. My choice to investigate the experiences of these improvisers using an interpretive phenomenological design aligned with the research question, which sought to gain insights on the participants shared experiences. The phenomenological design allowed me better to understand that the meaning of experiences do not reside in a single point or at a single instance in time, but rather result as a process and an evolution, which continue to influence the participants. Finally, the findings from this study imply that the practice by researchers of bridling permits them to balance objectivity and subjectivity while minimizing threats to credibility.

The participants provided me with many ideas of how colleges could include more theatrical improvisation opportunities on their campuses. As a result of the participants' belief that everyone could benefit from learning theatrical improvisation, these suggestions included adult education classes in the craft, academic classes in conjunction with the theatre or communications department, and splitting The Society into a performing troupe and a workshop group. Furthermore, the participants indicated that inclusion on future campuses of noncompetitive play (such as improv) rather than more competitive play (such as organized team sports) might help student activities departments on college campuses gain support from educational stakeholders based on the perceived positive influences on student development. The desire of the participants to share their experiences and their passion of the craft with me and the readers of this study speaks to their understanding of the role their experiences have had on their ongoing to development while outwardly presenting their experiences as "just being goofy."

Impact for the Reader

While some readers of this book may be improv actors or teachers of improv, more likely you are merely intrigued by the idea of improv being a factor to human success. Just as only one of the students in the study went on to pursue a career in the theatre, not everyone who thinks about and does improv needs to be a professional. Earlier, I spoke of the spirit of play. Not everything we do is play, but it makes things so much more fun if they have the spirit of play. Improvisation should be thought of the same way. In this way, improvisation should be practiced. One of the participants talked about needing to exercise it, as one would need to flex a muscle. From personal experience, I can say this is absolutely true. Since the completion of the study, I started practicing improv again. Although I have been teaching it for years and can see what is working and what isn't in others, I found I have lost the ability to jump into a scene and flow as I did back in my rainbow suspenders days. However, I am taking my own advice and being patience. This applies not only to skill development but also within scenes. Patience requires a person to listen, to watch, and yet still be engaged. Although some things come more easily for some, when it comes to learning, there is no magic bullet.

I also recommend failing. Failure has gotten a bad reputation over the years. It is through failure that we learn what works and what does not. Failure also indicates an effort to try. It is part of being alive. One of the things that are so attractive of video and computer games is the re-spawning, "do-over" aspect. Improv can be just as productive in failing. Most improvisers can recognize a scene that failed but rarely do they get hung up on it. Once the failed scene ends, they move on taking with them desire to do better next time. Here is where the concept of flow comes back in, if a person's skills are not up to the challenge the result can be anxiety unless the person can take the information from the failure to attain flow and make use of it. Additionally, if people never leave their comfort zones, they will also not achieve flow and the activity will be boring. While I am talking about improv, I'm thinking about how it shaped my life and how the participants in the study related how it influenced their development. Within the context of education and learning, these ideas need to be brought forward or we might have a generation of people, who do not know how to think critically, create, adapt, or enjoy life.

Implications for Applied Improvisation

As I noted in Chapter 11, after speaking with the generous and supportive applied improvisation professionals, I want to call for a bit of cohesion within the field. To the person, all the interviewees felt torn or "on the fence" about whether the profession of applied improvisation should have a standardization or certification process. On the one end of the debate lie the magic, wonder, and joy all the applied improvisers felt about their craft. On the other end lie the responsibility to meet the needs of the group and provide a safe environment. Those who I interviewed wanted others who hear the calling of improv to leap with the wild abandon only improvisers can. On the other hand, as I have mentioned before, improvisation and therapy walk a fine line. Damage can be done even in the spirit of fun. Using the improv principle of making your scene partner look good, seems to be a potential safety net for the high flying applied improvisers. Using the idea, similar to the Hippocratic oath of doing no harm, of making the players, company, students, or whoever look good and helping them find the fun and transformative power of improv may be the only standardization needed. Time will tell. While applied improvisation is not a new profession, it continues to grow in recognition, credibility, and value.

At this point in this book from the data and themes I have presented, one should understand that improvisation has transformative power for not only the individual but also for the larger community. Applied improvisation can affect positive social change through its practice with small groups and larger communities in need of social healing. One of the applied improvisation professionals I interviewed for Chapter 11 spoke of a colleague she knew who works with the Red Cross training young doctors in the principles of improvisation so that they can better perform their duties as field doctors in times of crisis. Another colleague of the interviewee works to provide safe places to play in war torn and turmoil ridden areas to build trust and rebuild community. Examples such as these indicate the grand scale of positive social change that could be affected though applied improvisation.

On a smaller scale, the ideas of listening, of being present, of serving the scene, and of failing good naturedly can, also, have profound impacts. One applied improv professional had the following to say:

> After a workshop, I often see a closeness that wasn't there at the start. Improv breaks down barriers, and the result is that people are connecting on a deeper level. They are listening to each other more actively, with compassion. By listening and truly hearing another's ideas and striving to see how we can accept those ideas before we negate them, we build a more trusting community.

While basic skills such as listening and accepting and building on another's ideas may not sound revolutionary, I see change on the individual level as the pebble in the pond that starts the ripple of change. As I have done throughout the book, I equate improvisation with play. By adhering to the core principles and applying them to their lives, together, humans could play through their lives creating culture and strengthening the societal connections that make us the social creatures we are. Both the participants from the study and the applied improvisation interviewees noted a need for social competencies in our society. Applied improvisation provides the avenue for improving those competencies.

FINAL THOUGHTS

I argue that improv is playing, that playing is a flow experience, that life is improvised, and that through learning how to have fun through improvising make life more enjoyable. The idea of what our culture holds as the goal of education holds little room for enjoyment. Ultimately, the goal of education needs to be rethought, not just reformed. Perhaps, it is naive of me to believe that an investigation of improv might add a tiny voice in the conversation of what we as a country and a culture want our young people to gain from their education. I offer it as a step towards understanding through describing and interpreting the experiences of the students in this study. I have attempted to weave concepts of play, flow, and improv together to provide a framework and to add to the knowledge base from which other scholars, researchers, or concerned individual might draw. The task of educational reform is not easy. Each day more and more students become disenfranchised. With the idea of surplus psychic energy not being used, I believe it will be like water—find a way to be expelled and not necessarily the way we might wish. Improvisation could be the gift that offers this potential. The more that is understood about positive ways to expel psychic energy in a positive fun manner, such as improv, the happier and healthier we will be as a society, seriously.

Appendix A:
Study Protocols

INITIAL INDIVIDUAL INTERVIEW PROTOCOL

Thank you for agreeing to share your ideas with me about your theatrical improv experiences with the student group at college. I will be recording the interview with digital audio equipment, as well as taking notes. If you have objection to being recorded, please tell me now, and I will only take notes. All names will be kept confidential and pseudonyms will be used in the transcripts and reports. All data will be stored on my personal computer and hard drive for at least 5 years at which time I will delete the recorded material. I will be conducting open-ended questions in the hopes that you will feel comfortable enough to interject any ideas or thoughts you may have as we discuss different aspects.

1. For background purposes: How long have you been (were you) a member of the group? What is your connection to the college: are you a current student, past student, or other? If other, please tell me how you heard about the group and became a member?
2. Tell me as much as possible about your experiences with improv here at the college, such as practices, performances, or anything that comes to mind.
3. Follow-up questions will happen after the interviewees have exhausted the experiences they wish to share at this time.
4. Additional questions will address areas of development (i.e., personal, academic, or social) not initially detailed.

5. Describe your sense of competence in improvising. How do feel you are at improv? In what ways do you feel competent or what areas do you feel you need work?
6. How has your sense of yourself as a student or learner changed since you joined The Society? How did improvisation contribute to this?
7. How has your sense of yourself in general developed since improvising with the group?
8. How did improvisation contribute to this?
9. Tell me about any specific instances during practice or performance when recognized a moment of change in you.
10. Is there anything else you would like to share with me about your experience with The Society?

Closure

Thank you so much for your time and willingness to share your experiences with me. I will be sending you a transcription of the interview for you to review. I will be referring back to things you mentioned today in our next session. Additionally, I will check with you throughout the analysis process to verify my observations, interpretations, and conclusions. As you recall, your identity will be keep confidential; however, in the focus group you will be with the other participants. If you need, to contact me for any reason my contact information is on the bottom of the consent form you signed earlier. Would you like that information again? I will contact you to schedule the focus group and follow-up interview.

FOCUS GROUP PROTOCOL

Introduction

Thank you for agreeing to share your ideas with me about your theatrical improv experiences with the student group at college. I will be recording the focus group session with digital audio/visual equipment, as well as taking notes. If you have objection to being recorded visually, please tell me now, and I will arrange the recording devices to capture only audio. At any point during the session, you may ask to edit the recording or withdraw your approval to be visually recorded. All names will be kept confidential and pseudonyms will be used in the transcripts and reports. Visual data will be deleted after transcription and analysis. No images will be used in any reports. All other data will be stored on my personal computer and hard drive for at least 5 years at which time I will delete the recorded material. I will be conducting open-ended questions in the hopes that you will feel comfortable enough to interject any ideas or thoughts you may have as we discuss different aspects.

1. Since the last time we talked, what things have you reflected on or wanted to discuss more about your experiences with improv?
2. While we are in a group setting, I want to review some of the things I heard from the individual interviews and have you reflect on them and discuss them as a group.
3. What stands out, puzzles you, or surprises you about your group experience?
4. What are your thoughts on improv in a college education should it be part of the curriculum or as an extracurricular activity such as it is here? Why?
5. Is there anything else you would like to share with me about your experience with The Society?

Closure

Thank you so much for your time and willingness to share your experiences with me. I ask that you keep the information from this session confidential. I will be sending you a transcription of the interview for you to review. I will refer to things that were discussed today in our final interview. As you recall, your identity will be keep confidential. Additionally, I will check with you throughout the analysis process to verify my observations, interpretations, and conclusions. If you need, to contact me for any reason my contact information is on the bottom of the consent form you signed earlier. Would you like that information again? In addition, I will contact you to schedule a follow-up interview.

FOLLOW-UP INTERVIEW PROTOCOL

Introduction

Thank you, again, for agreeing to share your ideas with me about your theatrical improv experiences with the student group at college. I will be recording the interview with digital audio equipment, as well as taking notes. If you have objection to being recorded, please tell me now, and I will only take notes. All names will be kept confidential and pseudonyms will be used in the transcripts and reports. All data will be stored on my personal computer and hard drive for at least 5 years at which time I will delete the recorded material. I will be conducting open-ended questions in the hopes that you will feel comfortable enough to interject any ideas or thoughts you may have as we discuss different aspects.

1. Since the last time we spoke have you had any more thoughts on your experiences that you can tell me about?
2. Given what you have shared about your experiences (should be able to reference from transcripts) what elements of improv do feel have contributed to your development to adulthood?
3. The Society is a student organization here at the college, what suggestions or improvements would you make about improv on campus if you could?
4. Is there anything else you would like to share with me about your experience with The Society?

Closure

Thank you so much for your time and willingness to share your experiences with me. As you recall, your identity will be keep confidential. If you need, to contact me for any reason my contact information is on the bottom of the consent form you signed earlier. Would you like that information again? I will be sending you a transcription of the interview. I will continue check with you throughout the analysis process to verify my observations, interpretations, and conclusions. In addition, I will contact you should I need clarification on something we discussed and to verify that I am representing what you have said to your satisfaction.

Appendix B:
Improv Games and Exercises

As a basic requirement for any exercise, I ask that players wear clothes in which they can move, be barefooted or in shoes that can grip the floor, not chew gum, and remove any jewelry that could be damaged or hurt others. At the beginning of any session, I define the space: what is off limits and what area is the audience or the stage. I have included a reflection section only in games or exercises that I feel truly need it. This does not mean a leader cannot reflect on a game of tag; I just don't often do so. All of these examples I consider to be accessible to beginners and good reminders for the more experienced.

SOCIOMETRIC EXERCISES

Walking

Number of players: All/group
Origin: *Games for Actors and Non-actors*, Augusto Boal
Premise: The goal behind variations on walking is to take an activity we do every day and reexamine the process to make us open to different possibilities and ideas. Walking through the space helps people become accustomed to the environment and the other bodies in the room and begins the process of presence.

Instruction:
1. Basic Walking-Ask the players to move through the space at their own pace without making contact with another person, furniture, or walls.

a. Right Angles-Ask the players to make right angles turns whenever they need to change direction.
b. Walk backwards
c. Stop and fill the space-Upon the command to stop, players must fill the holes in the space so that their bodies equally fill the room.
d. Changing Rates-Ask the players to speed up or slow down.

Side coaching:

- "Feel yourself as you move through the room."
- "Make sure you do not run into anyone or anything else."

2. Walking with sociometrics-Through side coaching questions, ask the stopped players to answer the questions with their bodies. Questions should be non-threatening and begin to make connections within the group as well as inform the leader.

Side coaching:

- "Stop. Put you hand on the shoulder of someone who reminds you of a family member."
- "Put your hand on the shoulder of someone who you'd like to get to know better."

Step-in

Number of Players: All/group
Origin: Learned while taking Playback Theatre basic training
Premise: As in other sociometric exercises, this one allows not only the leader to ask questions and learn about the group but also gives group members the opportunity to pose their own questions.
Instruction: Ask all players to make a circle facing inward. Tell the players that you will be asking them to step into the circle if they feel they meet the question. Once the players have moved, those in the center need to make eye contact and take stock of the others in the center. Players on the outside should also note who moved and who did not. Questions should be non-threatening but also probing.

Sample questions:

- "Step into the center, if this is your first time with improvisation."
- "Step into the center, if you know why you were named."
- "Step into the center, if you like pizza."

Side coaching:

* "There is no right or wrong question."
* "Look at who is in the center."
* "If you don't feel comfortable answering the question, you don't have to move."

After several questions, ask the players to blend or meld. To do this, everyone comes into the center and makes physical contact with each other moving through and around each other. After a few seconds, have them come back to the circle.

Side coaching:

* "Think of your bodies as liquid. Move over, around, under each other."

After the first blending, tell the players they now may ask questions. No order should be given as to who asks, as in it shouldn't just go around the circle. Questions should come organically from the circle. Players will begin to feel connected and present. After a few more questions blend again. This exercise can take as long as you need to get a good sense of the group and its needs.

Line-up

Number of Players: All/group
Origin: Playback theatre training, but I believe its origins lie in Moreno's work.
Premise: Using their bodies, players show their responses to questions posed to them from the leader. Questions should begin as strictly informational and can change in order to probe into the needs of the group. Using their bodies helps players lower walls that their inner cops might be guarding. As with the other sociometric exercises, Line-up begins to create community through the experience of putting one's body on a continuum with the others in the group.
Instruction: Describe the room as being an imaginary line describing the question you are about to ask. For example, in determining who have traveled the farthest to get to the session, one corner of the room is the farthest away. The other corner is closest with an imaginary line marking differences in between. Then the leader would ask the players to put themselves on the line. For questions like this, I allow players to talk amongst themselves. For questions that require observation, such as tallest to shorten players, I ask the players not to speak. For questions that may be subjective, I

find it more insightful not to have the players speak. An example of this would be oldest to youngest. Since no one is speaking, players put themselves on the continuum as per their perception of the others.

Side Coaching:

- "Line yourself up as to your own perceptions."

Warm-up Games

Letters

Number of Players: All/pairs
Origin: Unknown
Premise: Players will be asked to use their bodies to create letters of the alphabet. This begins the process of warming up their bodies, getting them out of their heads, and getting them to make connections with their group.
Instructions: 1. Divide the group into pairs. If there's an odd number, make one group a threesome. Position the groups in a circle around the room. Starting randomly with one group, ask the pair to make the first letter of the alphabet (together) with their bodies standing up. Move around the room through the alphabet.
2. Ask the group to make a straight line. I ask the players to make the letters again in pairs on the floor to be viewed from above. After the first two players have made a letter, they get up and go to the end of the line to "feed" the letter making a line. If you are working with adults in dresses and suits, you may want to adapt this to standing rather than lying down.

Side coaching:

- "Try to partner with someone you don't know."
- "Try not think too hard on this."
- "Work quickly."

Knots

Number of players: All/group
Origin: Unknown
Premise: Most people are not used to making physical contact with each other and have personal space bubbles around them that act as barriers. This game asks players to get in and (respectfully, make contact with each other), and then solve a problem together.

Instruction: Gather the group in the center of the space. Reaching across, under, through…other players, each player needs to join hands with another player. Both person's hands cannot be connected to the same person; each hand should connect with a different player. Once everyone is connected their job is to untie the knot to the best of the group's ability. Players can switch grips but not disconnect and reconnect to allow another player through.

Side coaching:

- "Don't be afraid to step over or go under another player."
- "Work together."
- "Keep each other safe."

Link Tag

Number of Players: All/group
Origin: Unknown
Premise: Link tag is a variation on tag that makes people look for physical connections with each other for a sense of safety.
Instruction: Define the space and what is off limits. If there is an even number, the leader should stand out. If there is an odd number of players, the leader should join in. Have a volunteer be *it*. The rules of tag apply: if tagged, you become *it*. The rest of the group stands around the room in pairs with their arms linked at their waists and their outside arms forming a link. Safety for the runner comes from being linked onto one of the open side arms of a pair. The outside person who has not been linked to, disconnects and becomes the new runner. Pairs may not run (at least not at first).

Side Coaching:

- Sometimes *it* becomes tired. I break apart a pair and ask *it* and runner to become a new pair (giving *it* a rest).

Ideation Exercise

Number of Players: All/group
Origin: Former student of mine
Premise: A key aspect of improvisation is thinking (often very quickly) without judging yourself or others. This exercise helps to introduce the premise of ideation, which often leads into long form improv.
Instruction: Gather the group in a circle. Start a noun or a "get." The person to the leader's left must come up with the first word that pops into their head.

The next person gives a word he or she associates with the last word given (not the leader's word). This form of ideation is called serial ideation, linking one word to the next in series. The words will change very drastically around the circle.

Once the word has gone completely around, explain the idea of parallel ideation. Instead of coming up with a word only associated with the word before them, they must all come up with a word associated with the first word. At first, the words will be what I call first level ideation (e.g., dog, collar. puppy, etc.). Eventually, the words will branch out, (e.g., dog, hound, pester, dogfish, veterinarian, etc.).

Side Coaching:

- "Try not to think too hard."
- (For the parallel ideation) "Keep the first word in mind when coming up with your word."

Variation: After doing the parallel ideation around the circle, have them come up with words (one at a time) in random order. Ask them to remember not only their word but the word before came before them. In this way, the exercise becomes a memory game, as well. After all the players have given a word, start the sequence again using the same words to see if they remember the pattern. Let it complete the cycle several times.

For even more challenge, start a second-word cycle in this way (new words, new cycle). After establishing the second cycle, re-introduce the first-word cycle simultaneously.

Side coaching: "This is challenging. Don't worry if we mess up. We'll start again."

TRUST GAMES

Mirror

Number of Players: All/pairs
Origin: Viola Spolin, Improvisation for the Theater, p. 60; Augusto Boal, *Games for Actors and Non-actors*, p.129 I credit both Spolin and Boal with developing mirror exercises primarily because they are the sources I have used. However, mirror exercises have become a standard to any theatre program and have varied in any way imaginable.
Premise: Mirror exercises help players to focus on a task, truly observe something without judgment, and build trust between the pair of players.

Instruction: Two players face each other. Determine a random fact (who's taller, older, etc.) pick who will be first. The first player chooses a common activity performed in front of the mirror (i.e., teeth brushing, dressing, etc.) and starts performing that activity. The second player mirrors the actions of the first player. After a time, player switch roles.

Side Coaching:

- "Watch carefully and don't make assumptions."
- "Move normally, not faster or slower."
- "This is not a tricking exercise. Be true to the activity."

Variations: There are so many.

1. Players switch back and forth throughout the exercise of who is the mirror and who is the initiator.
2. Players stand up in pairs in front of the group without telling them who is the mirror and who is the initiator. The audience guesses the roles.
3. 3.Group mirror: One initiator in front of the group with rest of the group acting as that player's mirror.

Reflection: Ask why do such an exercise. Ask the players what value they see in the exercise.

Columbian Hypnosis

Number of Player: All/pairs
Origin: *Games for Actors and Non-actors*, Augusto Boal, p. 51
Premise: Boal argued that to begin the process of building community humans need to restructure the relationship of their muscles to their world. In a manner similar to variations on walking, Columbian Hypnosis helps players move away from routine and mechanization and become more attuned to themselves.
Instruction: In pairs (can be 3s if an odd number), one player starts off as leader. The leaders hold their hands palm outwards, fingers up, about 8 to 12 inches from the faces of the other player. As if hypnotized, the follower must follow the leader's hand and maintain the distance. Leaders should experiment with levels and can change hands to allow followers to move through legs or other obstacles. The goal is to get the followers to use and awaken muscles that have been forgotten through everyday practices. After a while, switch roles.

Side Coaching:

- "Challenge your follower."
- "Follower maintain the distance between your face and their palm."
- "No physical contact."
- "Challenge but don't be aggressive. Work as a team."

Variations

1. One hypnotist guiding two followers with both hands
2. Multiple hypnotists working in a group following and leading at the same time
3. Lead with a different body part, such as a foot

Reflection: Ask the group about their sense of responsibility as the hypnotist for the well-being of their follower. Ask the followers how it felt to move differently then they normally would and being out of control of where their bodies went.

PRESENCE EXERCISES

Exposure

Number of Players: All/divided in two groups
Origin: Viola Spolin, *Improvisation for the Theater* p. 61
Premise: This is a great beginning exercise for players who have a fear of public presentations or are new to improvisation.
Instruction: Divide group in half. Send the first group on stage to line up facing the audience. Tell them their job is to be watched and that the audience's job is to watch them. After signs of discomfort are visible, give group one a task such as counting wall squares, or bricks. This job requires them to focus and gives them a task on which to concentrate. Have them continue to count (to themselves) until all signs of discomfort are gone. Switch groups. With the second group, only give them a task if they show visible discomfort.

Side Coaching:

- "Your job is to be watched."
- "Audience, your job is to watch them."

Reflection: Asking probing questions such as how the players felt on stage, what changes (if any) occurred when they were given a task beyond being watched, how the groups differed (if they did). Make the connection, after reflection, that focusing on a task is the players' POC. Having a POC helps them focus and be more in the moment.

Change Three

Number of Players: All/one volunteer to be the "Changer"
Origin: Unknown
Premise: This is a fun activity that helps players get used to observing each other and being observed.
Instruction: Ask for a volunteer and have that person go up on stage. Let the audience observe them for 15 seconds. Don't tell them why with the first person. After the time's up, have the volunteer leave the room, go around a corner, somewhere out of sight and change three things about their appearance. When the player comes back in, through the raising of hands, the audience gets to guess the changes. This can be repeated for several times. The changes become more and more difficult to spot as the audience becomes better at observing.

ACCEPTANCE EXERCISES

Who Game

Number of Players: Two
Origin: Viola Spolin, *Improvisation for the Theater* p. 109
Premise: One player knows who both players are in the scene and the other doesn't. Through offers and endowments, the player who knows helps the other player become the other character. Both players need to accept the offers and build on them.
Instruction: One player goes on stage. I usually have that person sit in a chair. That player needs to remain neutral and open. The second player determines a relationship to the other player and the characters in that relationship without telling the first player. Through the second player's actions and dialogue, the goal is to get the first player to know who they are. Once the first player has established who he is, together both players wrap up the scene as the point of concentration has been achieved.

Side Coaching:

- "Show don't tell."
- "Don't jump to conclusions."

Reflection: Did the second player show or tell the relationship?
Variations: There is a multitude, just within Spolin's book.

Add-on Freeze

Number of Players: All/group
Origin: Unknown
Premise: Two things (at least) are at work here: acceptance and presence. Players need to be careful to support each other not try to push their own agenda or try to be funny.
Instruction: Start with two players. When leading beginning improv, I start with an add-on freeze game. I just want the players to get used to the convention of hearing *Freeze!* But not taking their focus away from the scene. Secondly, I want each player to try and justify a new character in the scene. Give the first two players a noun. They start a scene. After the scene and characters are established, another player shouts, "Freeze," and enters the scene. All players on stage freeze until the new player begins an action or speaking. The new player has to establish a reason to be there without overshadowing the scene or changing the original scene. All players maintain their characters throughout the game. I let a maximum of five players get up on stage.

Side Coaching:

- "Show don't tell who you are and what you're doing there."
- "Share the scene."
- "Don't change the scene. You are all the same people (or things)."
- "Try for different physical levels."
- "Support your fellow player."

Variations:
1. Add-on Freeze Change
Instruction: After freezing the players on stage and entering the scene, the new player completely changes the scene (new location, new characters, new problem).
2. Freeze Change: Two players on stage begin a scene. The leader freezes the scene. From their frozen position, the two players change the scene. No new players enter; the same two players continue to play until the leader tell them to end the scene.
3. Blind Freeze: Same as Freeze Change except place the group of players upstage of the two players on stage. Have them face the back wall. The farthest player stage left yells, "Freeze," when he or she feels the scene behind them has reached a good place. The new player upon turning around tags out one of the two players and starts a new scene. This continues until the entire back line has had a chance to play.
Reflection: What do you find helps with starting a new scene?

What Are You Doing?

Number of Players: All
Origin: Unknown
Premise: Simply to accept offers from other players without question
Instruction: Circle up the players. Ask for a volunteer to go in the center. Ask the group for a suggestion of an action (e.g., digging a hole). The player in the center begins performing that action. Anyone player from the circle enters and asks the player in the center, "What are you doing?" The player who started gives an action which is not the one they are doing. Immediately, the second player begins performing that action and the first player rejoins the circle. This goes on and on.

Side Coaching:

*   "Don't judge, just do."

Variations: Start with two players on stage, the rest line up on one side as a feeder line. Give the two players an action which they begin to perform immediately. Ask one player, "What are you doing." That player has to give an answer to justify his actions but not the original suggestion. Then the second player answers and they alternate with different justifications until one repeats or fails to come up with an answer. Whoever fails, leaves, and is replaced by the next player off stage with a new action.
Reflection: Ask the group about what happens to their bodies when they "mess up."

Two By There By Bradford

Number of Players: All/pairs
Origin: Augusto Boal, *Games for Actors and Non-actors*, p. 106
Premise: Failure is built into this game. It is a good starting place for a beginner to learn to accept and embrace failure and to support their fellow players in the scene.
Instruction: Players get in pairs facing each other. Players repeatedly count to three alternating between themselves. After a short time, instead of starting with the word, *one*, players begin with another word. The players continue to "count" using the substituted word for *one*. After a while, have them substitute a second and then a third word for the numbers. Here's the important point of the game. Have the players determine a gesture and a sound in celebration for failure. When either of the players makes a mistake, both need to celebrate the failure.

Side Coaching:

- "Revel in the failure."
- "It's okay to make a mistake."

Reflection: Ask them how it felt to celebrate their failures.
Variation: Instead of another word, substitute a sound and motion.

Appendix C: Additional Substantive Quotes

The Hook

It's... having fun is fun... having fun is... It really makes me feel great it makes me feel better about myself, it makes me feel. (Flynn)

Practice is always fun and it's where you pick up the basics of these skills. What it really comes down to is performing the skills you learn in practice in a high pressure situation. (Caine)

Yeah we never turn someone down or said, "You cannot be here." We welcome everyone...As we talked about in the focus group, it's an outlet, it's therapeutic, it's anything you want to call it to whoever is in there. It's different for everyone for their reasons. So if there is someone that just needs that outlet and they don't have anywhere to go, we just want them to come to improv, to help them out. It'll help with the troupe too. It's a win every situation, so that's just the way it is. (Caine)

At was at first just getting more comfortable failing in front of the same people and I felt like it can be like really, really scary, really threatening when you don't have the confidence and you are not 100% sure in your ability to not make the same mistake or to not make other mistakes in the future. I know I had like some social anxiety when I first started improvising. It would be terrifying when I would like go up, shut down a little bit, and then just go on autopilot. Maybe I would say something or do something, and it wouldn't make any sense. It wouldn't make for a good scene… it would be kind of the exact wrong thing to do, but I've noticed it… when you have people in the same scene that help justify and bring that in and take that mistake and turn it in into like a strength then that builds up a great deal of confidence. I noticed that in myself. (Flynn)

(On how to attract new members, particularly women) Apparently there were some new people last year; I saw some in the show. They said some of them quit. I think you have to attract them in pairs. Get a couple to come out to support each other so they don't feel isolated, if you could get two friends to show up that would be great. (Fox)

That (his first performance with The Society) was a lot of fun. I can't remember the last time I did a short form game… it had been a long time…I mean I do them and practice them, but never in performance. Mostly because I like long form better. (Fox)

The Craft

It teaches you how to play with another individual, and it teaches you how to communicate. (Donnie)

You learn how to formulate a joke and you learn how to tell a story. You learn how to be present, how to listen, how to let go, and how to say, "Who cares!", how to be vulnerable, how to let go of yourself for second. I think all these things are lessons that our society desperately needs to learn. (Donnie)

It teaches you how to think on your feet, which is a very important skill to have. It teaches you how to get along with people and how to continue on with ideas…. which is just …it's a skill that is hard to learn elsewhere. (Caine)

The troupe itself takes it very seriously, like we take improv seriously, such a weird contradiction. I mean, we are serious about improv and just doing it making people laugh, having a good time, having fun in general whilst still keeping…the structure, finding out how it works and building as a team…so…. it's a weird area but it works. (Caine)

You try not necessarily say, "yes and," but it's more that you go along with the scene. You don't fight the scene. One of the improv members describe the scene as a river. You are able to guide yourself through the river as it is flowing, but it flows in a direction. You don't want to fight past that. (Briscoe)

A lot of people get used to getting taking themselves really seriously, and that's their rock. But that's not really true strength in that regard because those people are really inflexible. They can't roll with the punches; they can't adapt and improv teaches adaption. It teaches you to move forward and progress through a conflict and obstacles. (Freddy)

We did have a bit of difficulty from the theater department and like I said…the differences in theater are such that a lot of Shakespearean trained actors just are not interested in improv or performing it for one reason or the other. They think that their craft is superior, and there is a not a lot of intermingling. Otherwise, everybody at school generally likes us and sees the value in us and enjoys what we do even though they don't try it themselves. (Freddy)

I think it's, I think it's the closest you get to being a kid again. It's the same process children do… it's just that now you understand all the underpinnings of why it works. I don't think it's any different from what we do on stage than what small children do with action figures or when they put on a cape or anything like that. In fact, I guarantee you can probably teach kids some of these improv rules and their play would be better. (Donnie)

He (Donnie's first theatre professor) was absolutely phenomenal. He believed in what we were doing (teaching ourselves improv), and he loved it. He told us, "This is going to be the best acting training that you ever had." And he was right; he was 100% right. I wish that we were as important as the other art (scripted theatre). It's really the same thing. (Donnie)

I also think, in general, improv troupes should be more respectful of themselves. I think that they should take it seriously, and I also think they should work hard to do the best thing they can do because what you do affects everyone. When people go see a show that may be the first time they've ever see improv, I think this goes for all troupes including my own, it could always be better. It can always be more professional, and I think both sides need to view it as the art, as the beautiful, wonderful, scary, dirty, gross, awesome art that it is. (Donnie)

It (a performance) was a lot of fun. I remember getting the list of games… So much of improv is not the show. It's preparing for it and backstage, people being little nervous. I hope I am still nervous; I think that's a good thing. It's so much fun to be in the show. … it brings you together as a group. I guess, knowing that you have this thing ahead to do with the group. The success depends on everybody working together very well. (Fox)

I think the chemistry in The Society just developed over time come, over all the practices. A couple months leading up to the performance, people were getting to know each other. I didn't know they pretty much all knew each other and that I was a newcomer. I did not know if I would be accepted…I'm a lot older than they are, and they're all short form improv. I didn't know, cause I have a long form background, if they would want to hear what I would say. But then they got to know me, and they all seem to like performing with me so it's built up over time. For me, with some of my other groups, a lot of team building happens after practice. (Fox)

When I first got start interviewing for jobs in the Midwest, I picked up a local free paper. I never knew they were improv classes. I thought it was kind of funny, and I was too scared to do stand up and get out there by myself. I never heard of classes, and I remember reading these classes then I started taking classes. I think one of the reasons I got started was because I thought it would make it easier to talk to people. (Fox)

Everything is *yes and*, don't deny, I've had that drilled into me from the different schools. Also, focusing on the "who, what, where"; the relationships; playing on the top of your intelligence. I was taught to use slow and intelligent humor. Slow, in a good way not as an insult, intelligent humor that's when you let the humor build up over time, then it really pays off. (Fox)

That's a true thing. That it is about truth in comedy which is the name of the book, *Truth in Comedy*. So, so many things that I say in a scene are true, or they are based in truth, or they are believable. II had that drilled into me in training. (Fox)

Humor in recognition. Did you see the movie, *Karate Kid*? Do you remember sand the floor, paint the fence, and he's like, "I'm just fixing up your damn house; you're not teaching me any karate." He didn't see how the training would teach him karate. That's what these games are like in improv. Especially if you told a kid they were going to do improv to build to something bigger. They just want to have fun; they don't see how these would connect and help you build scenes down the road. (Fox)

I think people become sharper by doing improv. So much is creativity and seeing the relationship between two seemingly unrelated things. That is what creativity is—really seeing things in a different way and seeing the connection between unrelated things. (Fox)

For improv, it is about knowing different things. I think that is why not being an actor, I was able to do well. I knew lots of unusual things. I know I am supposed to say, it is acting. I guess what I am doing is actively acting. I'm playing something else; I'm an actor. I'm just not a good actor. (Fox)

The Rewards and Applications

Everybody in high school should be required to take an improv class. (Donnie)

I think it should be required because I think it teaches you how to play with another and individual. I think it teaches you how to communicate. There is a book that's called like everything I need to learn for life I learned in kindergarten. I think that's BS; everything that I ever needed I learned in improv. I've seen so many individuals that are socially awkward that have trouble communicating and have trouble talking to people or being in front of people. You give them six weeks of improv, and they're totally different people. It's like you learn how to formulate a joke, you learn how to tell a story, you learn how to be present, how to listen, how to let go and say who cares, how to be vulnerable, how to let go of yourself for second…I think all these things are lessons that our society desperately needs to learn that I think are probably socialist to some degree…but they're lessons. It teaches you how to cooperate with someone to a point where they could be going in a wrong direction and you don't care. You're thinking that whole time you're going to wrong direction, as long as we're in the wrong direction together, that we're okay. I think that there is a bond that you make with people that you don't experience other places. I feel like it's literally is good for the development of individuals, and I can be selfish because I feel like I learned so much from it. But I don't see how you can't. I don't think there's a single individual that cannot learn from this and cannot do improv and get better. People who tell me about improv…. oh you are rehearsing improv…it's not really a thing you just show up and you do it, improv is just a skill you either have it or you don't … That is part of the problem is that they don't understand that you can learn how to create things immediately and be better at it than you used to be. Why do we take classes like history? Take improv. This matters. This is important. This helps you. So many guys I know don't know how to talk to girls. All they really have to do is just be present in that moment that they have with a girl. In general, I feel like we would have a lot less people concerned about the way they looked and more people that are just living. (Donnie)

Everything that I ever needed, I learned in improv. (Donnie)

I feel like it's literally is good for the development of individuals, and I can be selfish because I feel like I learned so much from it. But I don't see how you can't. I don't think there's a single individual that cannot learn from this and cannot do improv and get better. (Donnie)

It was very central to the way my character developed as a person. (Flynn)

It's really peeling away layers, and it's not as complex as people think it might be, you can practice being funny but you also learn that funny happens, funny is not necessarily aiming for something particularly profane, or this or that. It's just pointing out the humor in general situations and funny situations just arise on stage. It's really a support system as well. You're not trying to stand out in front of your troupe mates; you are building something along them. We don't all succeed, then nobody succeeds. (Freddy)

When you're really, really good at improv you're able to creatively look at these problems and in a matter of seconds come up with ways to overcome them. I think that in a way, once you get really good at that you can transpose that into the real world…you're able to take something that sucks, like work, and you're able to solve problems in more creative way. You are able to have more fun because you can enter a scene at any time. You can take something that sucks and make it fun and make it easier for you to process and overcome and solve the problem. (Briscoe)

Most people say taking a communications class, speech writing class is one of the most difficult anxiety ridden experiences in their life. A lot of people don't like speaking to other people. A lot of people don't like getting up in front of other people, and I think that that shows that those muscles aren't very often flexed. (Freddy)

I think community education would be a good place to start. I think improv teaches a lot of social skills and a lot of ways to make you more personable with other people. That can affect how you do in college; it gives you the confidence to ask questions when you need to ask a professor or make friends to help you. It helps you to be able and confident to talk to one another. (Caine)

It makes it sound really depressing, but it's not, it makes my life worth living…It's my creative outlet. I get to come here and do my crazy thing, and no one judges me. (Lester)

I think it helps you with public speech. I am not intimated by talking in groups anymore. I actually took a speech class here (at the college), and the professor called me at home and told me I didn't have to take the final...."You got an 'A'." I said, "Yes!" (Lester)

As far as academics, I can say that it helped me a little bit in the ways that it just kept me going...I had to keep my grades up to keep going. It was more or less motivation that helped me ask the questions I needed. It helped me to become a little less shy and ask the teachers questions. (Caine)

Academics... I will admit that I am not the best student; however, I think that you're able to make school fun. If you're interacting with a lot of people in a group project, you're able to open up your imagination. Take something you know will be boring, like for me, math. Math for me has probably been my hardest subject...but being able to goof around, get people together, and work on something maybe you're not as good at. They are more comfortable with you with your, you know, confidence...so maybe not directly with academics but at the very least helping you be able to make something that wouldn't necessarily be fun a bit more entertaining. (Briscoe)

I guess with improv you do things in a more creative way. In real life, there are plenty of situations where you have to think on your feet and when you get a situation thrown at you that you weren't prepared for. Being able to feel confident in those situations I think has helped me a lot in my life. (Briscoe)

I mean as far as social development goes, confidence helps you across the board. Feeling confident enough to walk up and talk to someone, I think is completely thanks to my experience with improv. (Briscoe)

I think you become more confident, more outgoing. You are less afraid to be up in front of people like when you are in a group. I have seen so many people grow. People become more outgoing. I heard so many people take it (improv class) because they're shy. (Lester)

You need some fun in life...It releases endorphins. There was improviser in the Midwest, he was saying how terrified he was and that he would be on the verge of tears because of one improv teacher. It's not the right place for it, but fear does happen...That was a thing we used to be told by another instructor, "Follow the fear, follow the fear...go out follow your fear." But that's different from making someone cry. It about conquering your own fear, and It's about fun. Especially since nobody here is going to make any money doing it. (Fox)

Improv is both playing and learning. I learned by watching other people say something people know stuff about things. Kids are natural improvisers, let's pretend this, let's pretend that…that is improvising. (Fox)

The Continuance

It's good that this art form stays alive for people with short attention spans like me…. (laughs) because they can just do it whenever they feel like doing it. You don't need anything. It's free; all you need is a space. You can do improv anywhere. It is good for you developmentally, for your brain. It's good socially. If you have that fear being in front of people, it's good for you. It helps you vent out ideas. It is a great stress reliever; you get to laugh. If you laugh a lot, I heard you live longer, which is good or bad (depending on how you look at it). I think it is good. It's super important; it's super important. (Lester)

I feel like the people who do come to the shows and support us, they take us seriously in that sense but in order to take us seriously they still also have to have kind of an understanding that we are trying to make them laugh so it's being serious about being goofy. (Caine)

I've never seen it this way before. Apparently it's common in colleges—this weird divide between theater department and improv. (Briscoe)

I mean definitely talking about it…talking about the organization when you brought it up, really got me thinking about it more and more. I think this research sparked motivation to change it for the better and definitely remember that I left the group discussion way excited, more excited than I have been for improv just being able to talk about everyone's experience with it …getting into the mind of how people view improv… like it got me excited about it. Because I mean I love improv no matter what…this group on campus has been a love/hate kinda thing. I think just talking about it, what really got us into it, how we see it, it started back up that just being passionate about it in general…so I remember just have a great practice after that group interview. Just having, you know, being excited going in and having fun with that. It makes me want to work harder with it. (Briscoe)

Since doing these interviews, I respect my other improvisational actors even more, which is weird because I didn't know I could. But I think that I respect them even more. Hearing them talk about improv and hearing them in that group session hearing things that this has affected their lives in ways I had no idea… I think a lot of times I used to feel a much more alone in the way I think about improv. Knowing that they also have this life-changing experience and that I am a part of that even in a small way ...it's really touching...I think that it's an honor...I think it's an honor to be part of that. That night that we did that we all talked about improv in a group and then we broke off into rehearsal...we had a fantastic rehearsal. (Donnie)

We just need to form a better alliance with the drama department to reach into a different demographics but the demographics themselves, it's also just a function of chance. Originally, we had three or four females in the troupe and just much more varied group. Different people graduated, different people have moved away, and different people have gone off and formed their own troupes in other schools. That's really what's at play.... that is the running gag that were all white males now because we used to be much more varied but we're the only ones really stuck within the 15-20 mile range. We are really looking to reach out into the community of the college to pull in more varied groups so that everybody could benefit (Freddy)

As you get older, you are taught not to play, or you've got to keep score. I play in softball league; you keep score. It was just supposed to be fun; it just got so competitive. You are taught by the time you get out of college, and you start in the real world, you are taught not to show excitement, be under control. You're definitely not rewarded for playing. I am sure that there a certain companies or creative departments of ad agencies that still support play, but still you're gonna get your reviews and get judged competitively. (Fox)

They (other groups) do what we (The Society) do. You can't charge money, because you will kill Viola (Spolin), she'll roll over in her grave, if you do that. What we do here is closer to her idea of improvisation. In these big programs, they charge. I appreciate it when I come here to this group. I have fun, and I'm not paying. Usually, if you're in a group or you're the director, you've got to pay for the space to practice, you've got to pay for the space to perform. It's a very expensive hobby, or whatever you want to call it. People outside the college environment don't realize what they're getting for free, here. This is like really $500 worth that you get every semester. I shouldn't have said that because they are going to charge. Also I can't believe when I saw this online that anybody...anybody could come in, even alumni. You can't do that the other colleges. I think you've got to be a student there. It's not open... or if it's open, you audition, and then you pay all your dues. But I think this is as close to what Spolin had in mind when she first started it. (Fox)

QUOTES FROM APPLIED IMPROVISATION PROFESSIONALS

Background

I remember watching the British version of Whose Line Is It Anyway? (before it came to the United States) and thinking, "That looks like so much fun!" I wanted to join an improv class mainly for the fun. But what I found was so much more. I also had a huge fear of public speaking at that time, but by the end of every improv class, I felt I could talk in front of anyone. I felt so energized, centered, present, more alive, more in my authority, more in my confidence. I thought, "Now this is the magic!" I felt transformed. And I wanted to learn about what made it magic. Not only was it fun and creativity-enhancing, it completely transformed my ability to be with and in front of groups. (Michelle)

I was acting, I was teaching, and then I was also directing. It was when I was doing that work that a series of odd coincidences led me to an improvisation workshop. The story is too long of how I got there, but I went to the improvisation workshop and it…yeah…It feels like that was the beginning of my new life. (Rebecca)

Principles

I work with people on reprogramming their relationship to failure. (Michelle)

This one is less frequently used, however it can be a powerful one. It goes against somewhat conventional wisdom of think outside the box and don't go for the obvious. I have applied this most in creativity workshops where I point out that someone's obvious is almost always perceived as creative by someone else. If we can point out things that seem obvious to us, usually it makes for a stronger conversation, presentation, and/or connection. (Chris)

In improv you become more adaptive, responsive, and co-creative. Most significantly, you develop a new relationship with the unknown. The unknown moves from being something threatening--so you rigidly hold to what's familiar—to something filled with new potential. You develop a more flexible, adaptive relationship, where the unknown becomes a creative resource…place of new possibilities. You go from vying for who's right to exploring what's next. Improv principles and practices allow you to do that. (Michelle)Improv touches on those core competencies and abilities that I find useful for groups and communities having constructive conversations with one another. Improv has some of the best exercises I know, hands down, for teaching people how to listen and also teaching people having "a-ha" moments their failures in listening. In particularly, improv helps people recognize when the "fight or flight" reflex and fear creeps into that sort of very basic level of communication and gets them to lay it back. It helps people listen more fully, and really listen to fully what's being said before jumping in with their view. An enormous amount of conflict resolution principles is really held in the principal of *yes, and.* (John)

Social Change

Well frankly I think it's the key to peace on Earth. If I'm honoring, respecting, appreciating, and accepting (even if I don't agree), then we can have a really valuable, productive dialogue, and solve problems together, right? If the leaders of the world were operating this way, we wouldn't be having wars. (Sue)

I start to see that the beauty of the absurd is that it is often a metaphor for something realistic. It's about uncovering what the truth is. If we don't allow ourselves to be absurd, because we're afraid of throwing out an idea or of failing, then we risk not uncovering a fabulous idea of something that could actually work. (Lisa)

There's a real need for core competencies in our society, for hearing one another, for listening to one another fully, and to work constructively together. (John)

In crisis, people often freeze up or have a difficult time making any choice. Being able to make difficult decisions and be able to live with yourself, that's part of what improvisation can train us to do. We use our own best judgment, go with our impulses at a gut level, and make good choices. (Rebecca)

Other Quotes

(On why improv might not be taken seriously) Theatre, for centuries, has been the bastard child of society. Actors are suspect; they're witches; they're gypsies; they're not trustworthy. Roving actors would come to town. They'd leave, and your daughter's pregnant (laughs). Actors are not to be trusted. The theatre has been dying since Shakespeare was writing, So, if theatre is the bastard child of society, then it absolutely makes sense that any aspect of theatre that's unique, such as improv, would be the bastard child of theatre. (Rebecca)

Applied improv allows you low-stakes, low-risk preparation for high-stakes, high-risk real-life situations. (Michelle)

Resources

ORGANIZATIONS

Applied Improvisation Network http://appliedimprovisation.network
The Association for the Study of Play (TASP) http://www.tasplay.org/

BOOKS

Beaudoin, M., & Walden, S. (1998). *Working with groups to enhance relationships.* Duluth, MI: Whole Person Associates, Inc.

Belt, L., & Stockley, R. (1989). *Improvisation through theatre sports: a curriculum to improve acting skills.* Seattle, WA: Thespis Productions.

Foundation, N. G. (1976). *New Games Book.* Main Street Books.

Fox, H. (2010). *Zoomy zoomy: improv games and exercises for groups.* New Paltz, NY: Tusitala Publishing.

Godin. (2012). *Stop stealing dreams.* Retrieved from http://www.squidoo.com/stop-stealing-dreams

Jones, J., & Kelly, M. A. (2006). *Improv ideas: a book of games and lists.* Colorado Springs, CO: Meriwether Pub.

McKnight, K. S., Scruggs, M., & Second City (Theater company). (2008). *The Second City guide to improv in the classroom: using improvisation to teach skills and boost learning.* San Francisco: Jossey-Bass.

Safran, L. (2013). *Executive presence-Improv style!* Princess Ellen Publishing.

Safran, L. (2013). *Reading and writing come alive: Using improvisation to build literacy.* Princess Ellen Publishing.

Salit, C. R. (2016). *Performance breakthrough: a radical approach to success at work.* New York: Hachette Books.

FLOW

TED Talk- https://www.ted.com/talks/mihaly_csikszentmihalyi_on_flow?language=en

SOCIOMETRICS

http://www.Blatner.com

IMPROVISATION GAMES

http://improvencyclopedia.org/

APPLIED IMPROVISATION PROFESSIONALS
(INTERVIEWED FOR CHAPTER 11)

Michelle James
The Center for Creative Emergence, CEO/Chief Emergence Officer
Applied Improv and Applied Creativity Facilitator/Trainer/Coach
http://www.creativeemergence.com/

Lisa Safran
Improv Consultants, President and Training Strategist
http://www.Improvconsultants.com

Chris Sams
BATS Improv @ Work
Chris Sams and Associates, Applied Improvisation Facilitator/Trainer
http://www.chrissamsassociates.com

Rebecca Stockley, BFA
Co-Founder BATS Improv, San Francisco, CA
Applied Improvisation Facilitator/Trainer
http://improvlady.com

Sue Walden
ImprovWorks!, Director and Professional Development Consultant
http://www.improvworks.org

John Windmueller, PhD
Washington Improv Theatre (WIT), WIT@Work Organizational Training Manager
http://www.witdc.org

References

Aho, J. (2006). *Playback theatre—Articles and books. Rules vs. spontaenity (sic)*. Retrieved from http://www.playbacktheatre.org/resources/articles-and-books/

Ainley, M., Enger, L., & Kennedy, G. (2008). The elusive experience of "flow": Qualitative and quantitative indicators. *International Journal of Educational Research, 47*, 109–121. doi:10.1016/j.ijer.2007.11.011

Amrein-Beardsley, A. (2009). The unintended, pernicious consequences of "staying the course" on the United States' No Child Left Behind policy. *International Journal of Education Policy and Leadership, 4*(6), 1–13. Retrieved from http://journals.sfu.ca/ijepl/index.php/ijepl/issue/archive

Ardley, G. (1967). The role of play in the philosophy of Plato. *Philosophy, 42*, 226–244. doi:10.1017/S0031819100001303

Arnett, J. J. (2000). Emerging adulthood: A theory of development from the late teens through the twenties. *American Psychologist, 55*, 469–480. doi:10.1037/0003-066X.55.5.469

Bakker, A. B. (2005). Flow among music teachers and their students: The crossover of peak experiences. *Journal of Vocational Behavior, 66*(1), 26–44. doi:10.1016/j.jvb.2003.11.001

Bergen, D., & Fromberg, D. (2009). Play and social interaction in middle childhood. *Phi Delta Kappan, 90*, 426–430.

Berk, R., & Trieber, R. (2009). Whose classroom is it, anyway? Improvisation as a teaching tool. *Journal on Excellence in College Teaching, 20*(3), 29–60.

Blatner, A. (2009). Sociometry: The dynamics of Rapport. Retrieved from www.blatner.com/adam/pdntbk/sociomnotes.htm

Blatner, A., & Wiener, D. (Eds.). (2007). *Interactive and improvisational drama: Varieties of applied theatre and performance*. Lincoln, NE: iUniverse.

Boal, A. (2002). *Games for actors and non-actors*. New York, NY: Routledge.

Bodrova, E., & Leong, D. J. (2003). The importance of being playful. *Educational Leadership, 60*(7), 50–54. Retrieved from http://www.ascd.org/publications/educational-leadership.aspx

Brown, S. (2010). *Play: How it shapes the brain, opens the imagination, and invigorates the soul*. New York, NY: Avery.

Burghardt, G. (2010). The comparative reach of play and brain. *American Journal of Play, 2*(3). Retrieved from http://www.journalofplay.org/issues/31/121-comparative-reach-play-and-brain

Burnard, P. (2002). Investigating children's meaning-making and the emergence of musical interaction in group improvisation. *British Journal of Music Education, 19*(02), 157–172. http://doi.org/10.1017/S0265051702000244

Caillois, R. (1958). *Man, play and games*. (M. Barash, Trans.). Urbana and Chicago: University of Illinois Press.

Chang, J. (2010). Hermeneutic inquiry: A research approach for postmodern therapists. *Journal of Systemic Therapies, 29*(1), 19–32. doi:10.1521/jsyt.2010.29.1.19

Crooks, V. (2007). Using improvisation training to enhance creativity and cohesion in diverse groups. *Conference Papers — National Communication Association,* 1.

Csikszentmihalyi, M. (1991). *Flow: The psychology of optimal experience.* New York, NY: Harper Perennial.

Csikszentmihalyi, M. (1997). *Creativity: Flow and the psychology of discovery and invention.* London, England: Harper & Row.

Csikszentmihalyi, M. (2000). *Beyond boredom and anxiety: The experience of play in work and games.* San Francisco, CA: Jossey-Bass.

Csikszentmihalyi, M., & LeFevre, J. (1989). Optimal experience in work and leisure. *Journal of Personality and Social Psychology, 56,* 815–822. doi:10.1037/0022-3514.56.5.815

Dahlberg, K., Dahlberg, H., & Nyström, M. (2008). *Reflective lifeworld research* (2. ed). Lund: Studentlitteratur.

Dayton, T. (2005). *The living stage: A step-by-step guide to psychodrama, sociometry and experiential group therapy.* HCI.

De Backer, F., Lombaerts, K., De Mette, T., Buffel, T., & Elias, W. (2012). Creativity in artistic education: Introducing artists into primary schools. *International Journal of Art & Design Education, 31*(1), 53–66. doi:10.1111/j.1476-8070.2012.01715.x

Dewey, J. (1910). *How we think.* Washington, DC: Heath & Co.

Dewey, J. (1916). *Democracy and education: Complete and unabridged.* New York, NY: Feather Trail Press.

Dewey, J. (2005). *Art as experience.* New York, NY: Perigee Trade.

DeZutter, S. (2008). *Cultural models of teaching in two non-school educational communities* (Doctoral dissertation). Retrieved from ProQuest, UMI Dissertation Publishing. (3332082)

Dietrich, A. (2004). Neurocognitive mechanisms underlying the experience of flow. *Consciousness and Cognition, 13,* 746–761. doi:10.1016/j.concog.2004.07.002

Duckworth, A. L., Peterson, C., Matthews, M. D., & Kelly, D. R. (2007). Grit: perseverance and passion for long-term goals. *Journal of personality and social psychology, 92*(6), 1087.

Foubert, J. D., & Urbanski, L. A. (2006). Effects of involvement in clubs and organizations on the psychosocial development of first-year and senior college students. *Journal of Student Affairs Research and Practice, 43*(1). doi:10.2202/1949-6605.1576

Fox, J. (1994). *Acts of service: Spontaneity, commitment, tradition in the nonscripted theatre.* New Paltz, NY: Tusitala.

Freire, P. (2001). *Pedagogy of the oppressed* (30th ed.). New York, NY: Continuum.

Gentile, D. A., Lynch, P. J., Linder, J. R., & Walsh, D. A. (2004). The effects of violent video game habits on adolescent hostility, aggressive behaviors, and school performance. *Journal of Adolescence, 27*(1), 5–22. doi:16/j.adolescence.2003.10.002Gesell, I. (2005). Practiced spontaneity: Using improv theater skills to help teams master change. *Journal for Quality & Participation, 28*(1), 4–7.

Gesell, I. (2005). Practiced spontaneity: Using improv theater skills to help teams master change. *Journal for Quality & Participation, 28*(1), 4–7.

Goldstein, T. R., & Winner, E. (2012). Enhancing empathy and theory of mind. *Journal of Cognition and Development, 13*(1), 19–37. doi:10.1080/15248372.2011.573514

Gray, P. (2011). The Decline of play and the rise of psychopathology in children and adolescents. *American Journal of Play, 3*(4), 443–463.

Gray, P. (2013). *Free to learn: why unleashing the instinct to play will make our children happier, more self-reliant, and better students for life.* New York, NY: Basic Books.

Hammersley, M. (2002). Action research: a contradiction in terms? Presented at the Annual Conference of the British Educational Research Association, England. Retrieved from http://www.leeds.ac.uk/educol/documents/00002130.htm

Harper, D. (2001, 2014). *Online etymology dictionary.* Retrieved from http://www.etymonline.com/index.php?term=school

Hat Trick Productions, Warner Bros. Television (Producers). (1998). *Whose line is it anyway?* Los Angeles, CA: ABC.

Huizinga, J. (1950). *Homo ludens: A study of the play element in culture*. Boston, MA: Beacon Press.

Jacobs, J. (2011). Teaching and live performance: Applied theatre in universities and schools. *Applied Theatre Researcher/IDEA Journal*, (12).

Johnson, A. (2004). No Child Left Behind: The emperor has no clothes. *International Journal of Whole Schooling, 1*(1), 8–12. Retrieved from http://www.wholeschooling.net/Journal_of_Whole_Schooling/IJWSIndex.html

Johnson, J. (2010). *Race to the Top has unique role to play in reforming schools for the future – ED.gov Blog*. Retrieved from http://www.ed.gov/blog/2010/09/race-to-the-top-has-unique-role-to-play-in-reforming-schools-for-the-future/

Johnstone, K. (1983). *Theatresports: Official rules and regulations* (handout). Calgary, AB: Loose Moose Theatre Company.

Johnstone, K. (1987). *Impro: Improvisation and the theatre*. London, England: Methuen.

Joos, A. (2012). Improvisation: An empirical study on improvisational action. *Teatro De Improvisació. Un Examen Empírico De La Acción Improvisatoria, 33*(106), 79–91.

Graham, S., & Donaldson, J. F. (1999). Adult students' academic and intellectual development in college. *Adult Education Quarterly, 49*(3), 147–161. http://doi.org/10.1177/074171369904900302

Kataoka, S., & Vandell, D. L. (2013). Quality of afterschool activities and relative change in adolescent functioning over two years. *Applied Developmental Science, 17*(3). Retrieved from http://search.proquest.com.ezp.waldenulibrary.org/docview/1400587752?accountid=14872

Kearney, J. (2010). Writing as an altered state of consciousness: Process, pedagogy, and spirituality. *The Journal of the Assembly for Expanded Perspectives on Learning, 16*(1), 67–78.

Koukounaras-Liagis, M. (2011). Can an educational intervention, specifically Theatre in Education, influence students' perceptions of and attitudes to cultural and religious diversity? A socio-educational research. *British Journal of Religious Education, 33*(1), 75–89. http://doi.org/10.1080/01416200.2011.523526

Koutsoupidou, T., & Hargreaves, D. J. (2009). An experimental study of the effects of improvisation on the development of children's creative thinking in music. *Psychology of Music, 37*, 251–278. doi:10.1177/0305735608097246

Lauer, L. M. (2011). Play deprivation: Is it happening in your school? Retrieved from http:files.eric.ed.gov

Lobman, C. (2003). What should we create today? Improvisational teaching in play-based classrooms. *Early Years, 23*, 131–142. doi:10.1080/09575140303104

Lobman, C. (2005). "Yes and": The uses of improvisation for early childhood professional development. *Journal of Early Childhood Teacher Education, 26*, 305–319. doi:10.1080/10901020500371353

Lobman, C., & Lundquist, M. (2007). *Unscripted learning: using improv activities across the K-8 curriculum*. New York: Teachers College Press.

Longo, C. (2010). Fostering creativity or teaching to the test? Implications of state testing on the delivery of science instruction. *The Clearing House, 83*(2), 54–57. http://doi.org/10.1080/00098650903505399

Magerko, B., Manzoul, W., Riedl, M., Baumer, A., Fuller, D., Luther, K., & Pearce, C. (2009). *An empirical study of cognition and theatrical improvisation*. ACM Press. doi:10.1145/1640233.1640253

Manegold, C. (1994). U.S. Sets voluntary standard in teaching the arts. *The New York Ties*. Retrieved from http://www.nytimes.com/1994/03/14/us/us-sets-voluntary-standard-in-teaching-the-arts.html

Maples, J. (2007). English class at the improv: Using improvisation to teach middle school students confidence, community, and content. *Clearing House, 80*(6), 273–277. http://doi.org/10.3200/TCHS.80.6.273-277

McGonigal, J. (2011). *Reality is broken*. New York, NY: Penguin Press.

Meyer, P. S. (2006). *Learning space and space for learning: Adults' intersubjective experience of improvisation* (Doctoral dissertation). Retrieved from ProQuest Dissertations and Theses. (304913478)

Milgram, R. M. (2003). Challenging out-of-school activities as a predictor of creative accomplishments in art, drama, dance and social leadership. *Scandinavian Journal of Educational Research, 47*(3), 305–315. http://doi.org/10.1080/0031383032000079263

Miller, T. (Ed.). (2010). *Games: Purpose and potential in education.* New York, NY: Springer Science+Business Media.

Miner, A. S., Bassoff, P., & Moorman, C. (2001). Organizational improvisation and learning: A field study. *Administrative Science Quarterly, 46,* 304–337.

Moreno, J. L. (2008). *The essential Moreno: Writings on psychodrama, group method, and spontaneity.* (J. Fox, Ed.). New Paltz, NY: Tusitala.

Nachmanovitch, S. (2010). *Free play: improvisation in life and art.* New York: Tarcher/ Putnam.

Nichols, S., & Stich, S. (2000). A cognitive theory of pretense. *Cognition, 74*(2), 115–147. http://doi.org/10.1016/S0010-0277(99)00070-0

Nigh, K. (2013). Seeing feelingly: A phenomenological inquiry into the mind/body experiences of six drama students. *Curriculum Inquiry, 43,* 641–669. doi:10.1111/curi.12029

O'Neill, B., Piplica, A., Fuller, D., & Magerko, B. (2011). A knowledge-based framework for the collaborative improvisation of scene introductions. In M. Si, D. Thue, E. André, J. C. Lester, J. Tanenbaum, & V. Zammitto (Eds.), *Interactive storytelling* (pp. 85–96). Berlin Heidelberg, Germany: Springer.

Pellegrini, A. D. (2009). Research and policy on children's play. *Child Development Perspectives, 3*(2), 131–136. http://doi.org/10.1111/j.1750-8606.2009.00092.x

Piaget, J. (1962). *Play, dreams and imitation in childhood.* New York: W.W. Norton & Company, Inc.

Plato. (1994, 2009). *The internet classics archive: Laws by Plato.* (B. Jowett, Trans.) Retrieved from http://classics.mit.edu/Plato/laws.html

Pruetipibultham, O., & Mclean, G. N. (2010). The role of the arts in organizational settings. *Human Resource Development Review, 9*(1), 3–25. http://doi.org/10.1177/1534484309342852

Rasmussen, B., & Gürgens, R. (2006). Art as part of everyday life: Understanding applied theatre practices through the aesthetics of John Dewey and Hans Georg Gadamer. *Theatre Research International, 31*(3), 235–244. http://doi.org/10.1017/S0307883306002203

Ribeiro, M. m., & Fonseca, A. (2011). The empathy and the structuring sharing modes of movement sequences in the improvisation of contemporary dance. *Research in Dance Education, 12*(2), 71–85. http://doi.org/10.1080/14647893.2011.575220

Ross, J., & Tomlinson, B. (2010). How games can redirect humanity's cognitive surplus for social good. *Computers in Entertainment, 8*(4), 1–4. doi:10.1145/1921141.1921145

Sandseter, E. B. H., & Kennair, L. E. O. (2011). Children's risky play from an evolutionary perspective: The anti-phobic effects of thrilling experiences. *Evolutionary Psychology, 9*(2), 257–284. Retrieved from http://www.epjournal.net/articles/children%E2%80%99s-risky-play-from-an-evolutionary-perspective-the-anti-phobic-effects-of-thrilling-experiences/

Sanguinetti, J., Waterhouse, P., & Maunders, D. (2005). Pedagogies on the edge: researching complex practice in youth and adult community education. *Studies in Continuing Education, 27*(3), 271–287. http://doi.org/10.1080/01580370500394252

Sawyer, R. K. (2000). Improvisation and the creative process: Dewey, Collingwood, and the aesthetics of spontaneity. *The Journal of Aesthetics and Art Criticism, 58,* 149-151. doi:10.2307/432094

Sawyer, R. K. (2003). *Group creativity: Music, theater, collaboration.* Mahwah, NJ: L. Erlbaum.

Sawyer, R. K. (2004a). Creative teaching: Collaborative discussion as disciplined improvisation. *Educational Researcher, 33*(2), 12–20. doi:10.3102/0013189X033002012

Sawyer, R. K. (2004b). Improvised lessons: collaborative discussion in the constructivist classroom. *Teaching Education, 15,* 189–201. doi:10.1080/1047621042000213610

Sawyer, R. K., & DeZutter, S. (2009). Distributed creativity: How collective creations emerge from collaboration. *Psychology of Aesthetics, Creativity, and the Arts, 3,* 81–92. doi:10.1037/a0013282

Schmidt, J. A. (2010). Flow in education. In P. Peterson, E. B. E. Baker, & B. McGaw (Eds.), *International encyclopedia of education* (3rd ed. [pp. 605–611]). Oxford, UK: Elsevier. Retrieved from http://www.sciencedirect.com/science/article/pii/B9780080448947006084

Senge, P. M. (2012). Creating schools for the future, not the past for all students. *Leader to Leader, 2012*(65), 44–49. doi:10.1002/ltl.20035

Senge, P. M., Cambron-McCabe, N., Lucas, T., Smith, B., & Dutton, J. (2012). *Schools that learn (updated and revised): A fifth discipline fieldbook for educators, parents, and everyone who cares about education*. New York, NY: Crown Business.

Shernoff, D. J. (2010). Engagement in after-school programs as a predictor of social competence and academic performance. *American Journal of Community Psychology, 45,* 325–337. doi:10.1007/s10464-010-9314-0

Shernoff, D. J., Csikszentmihalyi, M., Shneider, B., & Shernoff, E. S. (2003). Student engagement in high school classrooms from the perspective of flow theory. *School Psychology Quarterly, 18,* 158–176. doi:10.1521/scpq.18.2.158.21860

Spolin, V. (1987). *Improvisation for the theater*. Evanston, IL: Northwestern University Press.

Statler, M., Heracleous, L., & Jacobs, C. D. (2011). Serious play as a practice of paradox. *The Journal of Applied Behavioral Science, 47,* 236–256. doi:10.1177/0021886311398453

Stevenson, L. (2011). *Creating destiny: Youth, arts and social change* (Dissertation). Stanford University, Stanford, CA. Retrieved from http://media.wix.com/ugd/1982b2_ff513eae8f845cf79d3a4ec0271549b5.pdf

Stevenson, J., & Clegg, S. (2011). Possible selves: Students orientating themselves towards the future through extracurricular activity. *British Educational Research Journal, 37,* 231–246. doi:10.1080/01411920903540672

Stevenson, L., Limon, C. J., & Reclosado, T. (n.d.). Community-based afterschool and summer arts education programs: Positive impact on youth and community development. *Expanding and Opportunities,* 79–82.

Sutton-Smith, B. (2001). *The ambiguity of play*. Boston, MA: Harvard University Press.

Taylor, P. (2002). The applied theater: Building stronger communities. *Youth Theatre Journal, 16*(1), 88–95. http://doi.org/10.1080/08929092.2002.10012543

Teng, C. (2011). Who are likely to experience flow? Impact of temperament and character on flow. *Personality and Individual Differences, 50,* 863–868. doi:10.1016/j.paid.2011.01.012

Treff, M. E. (2008). *The essence of Participation Training: A phenomenological examination of graduate student experiences* (Ed.D.). Ball State University, United States -- Indiana. Retrieved from http://search.proquest.com.ezp.waldenulibrary.org/pqdtft/docview/304689897/A649E30DD8B6469FPQ/1?accountid=14872

Tuisku, H. (2010). Diving in: Adolescents' experiences of physical work in the context of theatre education. *International Journal of Education & the Arts, 11*(10). Retrieved from http://www.ijea.org/v11n10/

UN Convention on the rights of the child. (2005). Retrieved from http://udel.edu/~roberta/play/rights.html

Vagle, M. D. (2014). *Crafting phenomenological research*. Walnut Creek, CA: Left Coast Press.

Van Manen, M. (1990). *Researching lived experience: Human science for an action sensitive pedagogy*. Albany: State University of New York Press.

Van Manen, M. (2014). *Phenomenology of practice: Meaning-giving methods in phenomenological research and writing*. Walnut Creek, CA: Left Coast Press.

Vendelø, M. T. (2009). Improvisation and learning in organizations: An opportunity for future empirical research. *Management Learning, 40*(4), 449–456. http://doi.org/10.1177/1350507609339684

Vera, D., & Crossan, M. (2005). Improvisation and innovative performance in teams. *Organization Science, 16*(3), 203–224. http://doi.org/10.1287/orsc.1050.0126

Walker, C. J. (2010). Experiencing flow: Is doing it together better than doing it alone? *The Journal of Positive Psychology, 5*(1), 3–11. doi:10.1080/17439760903271116

Wenner, M. (2009). The serious need for play. *Scientific American Mind, 20*(1), 22–29. http://doi.org/10.1038/scientificamericanmind0209-22

Wiener, D. J. (1999). Using theater improvisation to assess interpersonal functioning. *International Journal of Action Methods, 52*(2), 51-53.

Zaunbrecher, N. J. (2011). The elements of improvisation: Structural tools for spontaneous theatre. *Theatre Topics, 21*(1), 49–59. doi:10.1353/tt.2011.0015

Zaunbrecher, N. J. (2012). Suspending belief and suspending doubt: The everyday and the virtual in practices of factuality. *Human Studies, 35,* 519–537. doi:http://dx.doi.org.ezp.waldenulibrary.org/10.1007/s10746-012-9244

Lightning Source UK Ltd.
Milton Keynes UK
UKOW04f2201011217

313672UK00001B/80/P